WIT...

GOOD GOODBYES

Starting school is just one of the many early—and challenging—goodbyes between children and their parents. This book is about those ordinary, everyday goodbyes: when you go out for the evening, when you go to work, when your child first goes to preschool or school. And the message is that... make the goodbye-head... this... program helps parents... good goodbyes... competence and confidence in young children.

Donated to
SAINT PAUL PUBLIC LIBRARY

NANCY BALABAN... is Director of the Infant and Parent Development... Bank Street College of Education Graduate School. A former preschool teacher and the mother of three, she is author of *Observing and Recording the Behavior of Young Children.*

LAWRENCE BALTER, Ph.D., is a Professor of Educational Psychology at New York University. He is the author of *Dr. Balter's Child Sense*, and the host of a number of nationally syndicated radio call-in programs for parents.

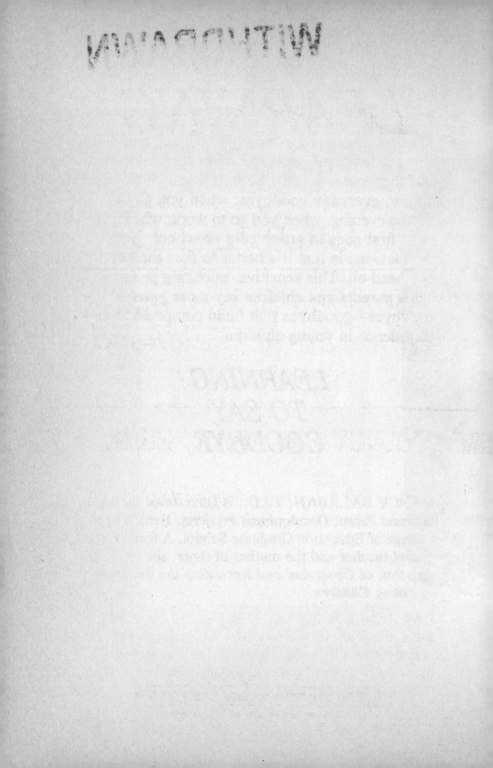

LEARNING TO SAY GOODBYE

Starting School and Other Early Childhood Separations

NANCY BALABAN, Ed.D.

With an Introduction by
Lawrence Balter, Ph.D.

A PLUME BOOK

NEW AMERICAN LIBRARY

NEW YORK AND SCARBOROUGH, ONTARIO

When my youngest daughter went to kindergarten, an event took place that caused her daily distress. The teacher, it seems, put Willie in the coatroom every morning because he cried for his mother. He was permitted back into the classroom when he stopped crying. Eventually, he learned not to cry for his mother.

This book is written in the belief that other solutions to Willie's crying can be found.

Acknowledgments

I would like to acknowledge the influence and assistance of a number of people.

New York University gave me the opportunity to do this work. Many students at Bank Street College contributed insightful anecdotal material. I appreciate the generosity of the teachers who allowed me to take photographs in their classrooms and the many parents who made important contributions.

I wish to thank the numerous children and parents with whom I have worked over the years for providing me with knowledge, fun, affection, and challenge. How could I have written this book without them?

Finally, this book could not have been realized without the insights of Dr. Henriette Glatzer and the support, encouragement, and understanding of my husband, Richard Crohn.

CONTENTS

INTRODUCTION

When I was five years old, my parents and I moved in temporarily with my maternal grandparents. For some reason, my parents decided to enroll me mid-year in a kindergarten class. I had never been to school before. I did not know the routines, and the teachers and children were unfamiliar to me. The entire experience was strange and frightening and in retrospect, I can only assume that my parents thought my life should continue as though nothing had changed. I realize now that feeling uprooted by the move made my adjustment to school even more difficult. Today we are much less likely to take children's feelings for granted and are more apt to understand the significance of transitions and separations in a child's development.

I think it is safe to say that children begin the long and challenging process of separation from their parents at the time they are born. Obviously the first separation is a physical one, marked by the severing of the physical connection between mother and child immediately following birth. Although the physical separation is abrupt, the psychological process of emotional separation is probably a lifelong endeavor. Normal psychological and social development is characterized by a gradual process of mental distancing from one's parents and primary caregivers. Emotional separation is necessary if a child is to develop a sense of individuality and wholeness.

Much of the process of psychological separation emanates from a healthy child's drive to become masterful and competent. In a normal course of events, children want to understand their environment and they strive to develop their innate potentials. Naturally there are occasions when they need our guidance and encouragement.

There are countless examples of children's daily efforts to become psychologically separate. In infancy, the ecstasy of the peek-a-boo game has long been thought to have significance in the separation process. It can be seen as an attempt to master the temporary loss of a loved one. The game is thought to represent separation and loss on the one hand, and the thrilling relief of being reunited on the other.

Many eight- and nine-month-olds show a wariness toward strangers that was not apparent at an earlier age. As they develop, small children gradually come to the worrisome partial realization that their parents are separate from them. It is as though the appearance of a stranger serves as an unwanted reminder that the emotional unity they wish to preserve can be disturbed by intruders.

At about the same age, infants often refuse to be fed. Sometimes parents take this behavior to mean their babies do not want to eat. Some resort to all sorts of intrusive efforts to force their children to eat. More often than not, however, their refusal to eat means children prefer to feed themselves. Occasionally they even gain pleasure from feeding their parents.

In toddlerhood, children seem to derive endless joy from running away from parents and squeal in delight when you catch them and swoop them up in your arms. This is another example of the continuing struggle toward separation and independence—made safe by the child's knowing that you are there to catch him. Much seemingly incorrigible and disobedient behavior is motivated by an underlying striving for individuality.

In toddlerhood we also witness the well-known negativism that has become associated with the phrase Terrible Twos and the endless repetition of the word "no" that threatens to drive you to distraction. This, too, can be interpreted to mean that the child is making an effort to separate himself from you. By drawing a line between what you are offering and what he is agreeing to, a child is emphatically stating that he is not you. The toddler makes a strenuous effort to show the demarcation between your thoughts and his—as if to convince himself that you and he are not the same person. "I'm me, and you're you" seems to be the predominant feeling during this stage of a child's development.

As children reach the preschool years a unique psychological process enters into the developmental scheme of things. Preschoolers begin to imitate you; they use your mannerisms, gestures, and even your gait. Frequently they will repeat an unedited version of one of your favorite phrases, complete with accurate syntax and inflection, and without the expletives deleted! This is referred to as the process of psychological identification. First, by imitating you, and later, by taking your characteristics as their own, children develop an internal sense of you. This enables a child to be alone without feeling abandoned. Identification helps a child to be physically separated for periods of time without becoming anxious or depressed, much the way a pacifier or security blanket serves to soothe and comfort a younger child.

Thus far, I have discussed the normal efforts on the part of the child to move away from his parents toward greater independence, but there are also separations not initiated by the growing child. Some of the more obvious examples of separations imposed on infants and small children are moving out of the parents' bedroom, weaning, toilet training, and being left with a substitute caregiver.

As I alluded to in my opening statement, for generations adults have trivialized children's concerns. Children were not always adequately prepared for important changes in their lives and it was thought that they would simply adapt to new situations. When they did not, they were regarded as problem children. Their regressions, fears, and sleep disturbances were misunderstood and not seen as symptomatic.

Educators and psychologists have gradually come to realize that we must help children and their parents with the separations they encounter in their everyday experiences. Going to school represents an imposed separation of enormous magnitude for a small child. There are unfamiliar people with whom they must interact, new rules and regulations to abide by, evaluations by professionals (not emotionally biased parents) to which they are subjected, and groups into which they must assimilate. All of these new experiences necessitate a great deal of self-control and courage.

On my radio programs and in my clinical practice I speak with hundreds of parents each month and I have often been struck with how parents themselves need assistance in their roles as helpers in the child's separation process. During the first day, perhaps even during the first hours after an infant's delivery, an intense emotional bond is formed between parents and their baby. Psychologists believe that this bond enables parents to cope with the demands of a helpless infant: the loss of sleep, the constant giving without receiving, the selfless devotion that is offered without a word of appreciation in return. At times, though, parents may find it difficult to support their offsprings' efforts to become separate people, i.e., to let them go. Parents can be either a help or hindrance in this difficult navigation from total dependency toward personhood status.

It is clear that parents and educators must collaborate in guiding children properly when the time arrives for a child to enter school. Nancy Balaban's book helps parents and children make transitions like the one from home to school smooth. Her readers are treated to practical suggestions designed to avert adjustment problems and to make school attendance the pleasant and rewarding experience it should be.

Lawrence Balter, Ph.D.
Professor of Educational Psychology,
New York University

LEARNING TO SAY GOODBYE

This is when my Mommy left me.

Michele

Chapter 1

SAYING GOOD GOODBYES

Are you able to remember your first day at school? A curtained kindergarten window, a sandbox, an unknown child with curly hair, boxes of large crayons, a shiny linoleum floor, the teacher's face or voice, fighting back tears as your parent left?

Even though these memories are veiled by many years, they are often available to us as adults, and often tinged with sadness.

Starting school is but one of many early—and challenging—goodbyes between children and their parents. A young child's life is filled with many different sorts of goodbyes. Look at two-year-old André, who has just had a precipitous goodbye thrust upon him:

André is standing with his mother and her friend waiting for an elevator. The friend is bidding them goodbye. The elevator arrives, the doors open, and André's mother steps in believing that he is following. The doors snap shut and André is left with the friend. He dissolves in tears when his mother disappears into the jaws of the elevator. Despite the

1

friend's calm reassurance that "Mommy will come right back," André is beyond consolation. After a few moments, the elevator reappears and coughs up his mother. André is ecstatic.

André believed that his mother had disappeared *forever* and then had magically reappeared. Had he been four or five years old, rather than two, he would have understood the working of the elevator and, though distressed, could have been reassured that his mother would be back immediately.

This book is about ordinary, everyday goodbyes that occur between parents and their young children: when parents go out for the evening, when parents go to work, or when children first go to group care or school.

The message in these pages is that it's better to face the goodbye head-on than to avoid it.

This is a tough message, for as we all know it's more comfortable to sidestep trouble than to march right into it. But is it good for children? The answer is a decided no—because when you've avoided saying one goodbye by sneaking away, there's bound to be another lurking just around the bend. In being devious, what you end up with is a child who doesn't believe you.

As a professional who has spent twenty years as a teacher of three- and four-year-olds, and the last fifteen years as an educator of teachers at Bank Street College, I have helped many parents and children say goodbyes to one another in ways that contributed to their strength. It was because so many teachers, and so many parents and children had difficulties with these daily partings—even when they tried to handle them well—that I decided to devote my doctoral dissertation to this topic. One of the results of that study was this book.

This book is designed to help parents and children say more *good* goodbyes—goodbyes that build competence and confidence in young children.

Some Everyday, Ordinary Goodbyes

Young children experience a variety of daily separations even though they actually remain in the same physical space with you. Going to sleep is probably the most familiar form of separation. Babies say a temporary goodbye when they are put to sleep in their cribs—goodbye to you, goodbye to their toys, to the room, to the world. Three- and four-year-olds sometimes have the notion that when they close their eyes to go to sleep either they, or you, disappear. Sleep becomes a separation that some children find difficult to tolerate. This is especially so during the toddler period when babies are so excited by the discovery of the world "out there" that they despair of saying goodbye to it.

Your young baby probably "says" hello and goodbye to you all during the day as you pass from one room to another in your home. You may find yourself greeting each other with smiles, coos, or "hi's". Maybe you chirp "I'll be right back" as you go to fetch a bottle or a clean diaper. Perhaps there are peek-a-boo games that you play behind a blanket, behind your fingers, or over the end of the crib. These, too, are separation experiences—rehearsals for the real thing.

Toddlers, those runabout babies, have even more frequent separations once they are mobile. They wander into the bedroom and realize that you are still in the kitchen. A cry goes up, a call for help. Mommy! Daddy! Where are you? Even though it was the toddler who left you, she somehow thinks it was you who left her.

Sometimes you want privacy in the bathroom. "Wait here," you say, "I'll be right out." You close the door. Unearthly screams and pounding emanate from the other side of the door. The toddler isn't at all sure that you are really in there or that you will ever come out. Part of this is due to the toddler's undeveloped sense of time. Two seconds are frequently experienced as two weeks, thus the toddler's panic and sometimes ineffectiveness of your words.

There are many other daily commonplace goodbyes that contribute to young children's developing ability to cope with the appearance and disappearance that characterize all separation experiences. Here is a beginning list. Perhaps you can add many more:

- Outgrown clothing is given away or "handed down" to a younger sibling.
- A crib is put into storage (or given to the new baby) when the "big bed" is acquired.
- The high chair is removed in favor of a booster seat at the table.
- The bottle, or breast, is replaced by a cup.
- A favorite blanket, diaper, or soft toy "security object" is lost.
- Supper is consumed; a ball rolls under the couch; a squirrel in the park scampers up the tree into the leaves, and baby says "All gone!"

Sometimes in the course of everyday living, "goodbye" events occur that cause minor upset. You are in the supermarket and your young child wanders off among the vegetables while you are engrossed in the meats. You are walking down the street and momentarily drop your child's hand. He grasps a hand again and looks up to discover that he has latched on to a complete stranger. His face registers panic and confusion.

Separations take many forms. Very young children often think that when their mother or father puts on a hat that the parent has disappeared and another person has taken their place. They may cry or look bewildered. Sometimes they believe that their parent has been replaced by a stranger by virtue of a haircut. One three-year-old watched his fully bearded father being shaved by a barber. When the smooth-faced father turned to look at his child, the youngster said, "You used to be my father and now you're my mother, right?"

More significant separations take place when you leave children with substitute caregivers in your own home. Sometimes you may be gone for short periods—to the movies or to a meeting. Sometimes for longer periods—to work, on a vacation, on a business trip, or to have a baby. Other important separations occur when a caregiver who has been a steady person in the young child's life leaves and a new caregiver comes to take that place. Careful, calm explanations to children before these events occur will help provide them with the inner strength needed to cope.

In schools and child care centers, separations from people other than their parents are also very meaningful to children. A teacher leaves to have a baby or take another job. Children move to another classroom with a new teacher, leaving their former teacher in the old room. Children leave their center and go to a different program for the summer. Children leave nursery school and go to kindergarten, described by one author as an "abrupt and permanent break with the past."[1]

These ordinary goodbyes provide opportunities for you to have an impact on your child's growth. When you give children clear explanations, you prepare them for separation events and build their trust in your reliability. Children count on us for the *truth*. That is one way that children develop some control over their lives.

Children's Feelings: Laughter and Tears

Separation from parents* or from primary caregivers frequently makes young children unhappy. They often feel abandoned, cast aside, and uncared for. They may be frightened and just as often angry. Sometimes children scream and cry. They throw things. They hit other children. They may try to hit the teacher. They bite. They kick. They lie on the floor and have temper tantrums.

Sometimes the situation is very different. A child walks into the classroom as if she belongs there, as if she has been there a thousand times before. She handles the equipment. She plays with other children. She blithely waves goodbye to her parent. She speaks in a friendly way with the teacher. "What a great kid!" the teachers remark. "No problems at all," the parent says, "she just left me and got really involved in the activities." Then one day, her mother leaves as usual and the girl collapses in a torrent of tears. No one can console her. She wants no part of any activity. Her behavior is completely unexpected. Her teachers feel bewildered and frustrated.

Other children may hide their feelings even more.

*The term "parent" is used in this book to denote the person who is the primary caregiver for a child, such as a mother, father, grandmother, aunt or uncle, older sibling, or foster parent. The words "school" and "center" are used to indicate a range of settings, including infant and preschool day-care centers, nursery schools for three- and four-year-olds as well as for toddlers and two-year-olds, and kindergarten.

Children who feel sad or troubled about leaving the person or persons to whom they are attached do not always make those feelings known.

They appear quiet and nonassertive. They seem to walk parallel to the life of the classroom. Often they are overlooked because they do not cause trouble. They seem self-sufficient and unassuming. A closer look may reveal that they are not involved with the materials of the program or with other children to any significant degree. A teacher might think that such a child is mildly unhappy or has a low-key disposition. The parent may say he does not act that way at home. Such a child might be physically at school but psychologically at home.

Children respond differently to the newness and the strangeness of an unfamiliar place. Some become agitated and race around the room, poking, prodding, touching, and looking. Others seem to be uncomfortable; they hang back and explore with their eyes while their bodies remain inert.

Not every child who comes into a classroom is affected in these adverse ways. Some march in full of confidence and behave as if they naturally belong in the room. For them, and their parents, the first day of school may be the culmination of a summer of anticipation or the reality of a longed-for adventure, shared originally, perhaps, with an older sibling. Some may be quite used to school or group care through prior experiences, although children who did not work through their separation feelings the first time may still have difficulty. Others seem to enjoy the novelty of the situation, the excitement of being with other children their own age, and the pleasure of new play-

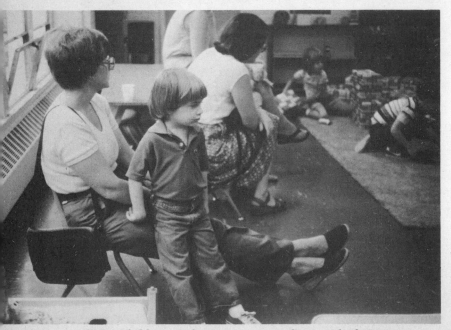

Some children explore new surroundings with their eyes.

things. However, most children react vigorously in some way to new surroundings, though that reaction may go undetected. It seems that children do mental and emotional work to absorb and understand a novel setting.

Children need to size up the human environment as well as the physical environment when they enter a new classroom. The teacher becomes an object of intense interest and curiosity. Children may wonder: Does the teacher speak my language? Is the teacher my color? Are any of the teacher's mannerisms or attitudes familiar? Are the teacher's reactions to my behavior like my parents' reactions?

Factors like these contribute to a child's sense of strangeness or comfort because young children tend to define the whole adult world in terms of the behavior of their own parents. Children often expect that all adults will behave as their parents do. For example, if mother leaves every morning in a rush to catch the bus and father cooks breakfast while singing, chances are that the young child believes that all mothers and fathers do that in the morning. If mother does not allow water play in the bathroom sink, the child may believe that all mothers prohibit this sort of play and might even be surprised at the mother or teacher who allows it. It takes time and new experiences with a variety of adults to teach them that adults behave in many different ways.

Because they enter school with these preconceived notions about adults, children may be very uncomfortable as they begin to perceive that the teacher does not behave like their mother, father, or grandmother. Perhaps the teacher says it is fine to play with water, or talk while you eat, or get your hands dirty with glue. Children need time to put this new category of adult into their working intellectual scheme.

When a child trusts, she transfers her loving feelings from parents to teachers.

They need time to differentiate between what goes on at home and what goes on at school. They need time to learn about the teacher, to learn what certain tones of voice mean, and to learn what to expect in various situations. They need time to sort out the differences between their teacher's and parents' behaviors. If the teacher is a benign and caring person, a child who is ready for school or group care will be able to transfer feelings of "basic trust"[2] from home to school.

Until children come to feel this sense of trust, however, the teacher and the classroom remain strange. Day by day, familiarity replaces the unknown. This gradual process begins with the relationship between teacher and children. As children perceive the teacher in ever more trusting terms, they often begin to expand their relationships to the physical environment and to other children. Establishing comfort with the teacher as a base enables children to become comfortable with the whole classroom.

Research has revealed a similar process in infants.[3] Babies, it seems, first need to know that people are trustworthy and here to stay. They gradually learn that mother is not out of the world when she is out of sight. After that, babies are able to extend that concept to the physical objects in their world. It is by means of consistent, intimate human relationships that children become related to the larger physical and human world.

Children may feel strange in a new group that is unlike the familiar family group in which they have a special status. In the new group, few people know their names. No one knows whether they like vanilla ice cream or chocolate, or what frightens or comforts them. No one really likes or dislikes them in any particular way. They do not have a natural place in this group but will have to earn it, through their behavior. While they do not know any of this yet, perhaps they sense it.

Children may worry that no one will take care of them, that they will not know how to get home, that they will not be able to find their parents, or that their parents will not be able to find them. The younger the child, the more intense these feelings of fear. Some researchers conclude that until children are around three years old, they cannot retain a stable inner mental image of their absent parents.[4] Words or explanations of parental whereabouts are often ineffective with such young children until they trust the new adult.

The way children approach separation may also be determined by their particular family style. One family may be flamboyant; goodbyes and other emotional events may be treated in a demonstrative fashion. Another family may be more reserved; their feelings are not openly revealed and meaningful events are handled with outward composure.

Parents' Feelings: Excitement and Fear

Sometimes we may feel that it is not the child but the parent who is having trouble separating. Surely a child's feelings are intimately bound up with those of his mother or father. Parents may have various kinds of emotions when they bring their children to school for the first time. It is not possible to understand a child's feelings without simultaneously acknowledging our own feelings.

Parents may wonder: Can the teacher really take care of my child? Will the teacher understand him when he makes requests? Will the teacher like her? What will the teacher do if my child misbehaves? Will he humiliate me or enhance me in the eyes of the teacher? Will she reveal things about our family that are private? What will happen if my child gets hurt in school? Can I really trust this teacher with him? These nagging questions make it difficult for some parents to hand over their son or daughter to a teacher's care.

Parents may worry about how their children will get along without them or how they will function without parental control, guidance, or protection. In

Parents and children have strong feelings when they bid each other goodbye.

situations where parents have not left their children outside the home before, this feeling may be particularly strong. In some cases, it may be less worrisome if this is a second or third child. Alternatively, a parent may expect the separation to go more smoothly with a second or third child and that may not be the case. However, more depends on a child's personality and relationship with the parents than on the birth order.

One source of this worry may be parental ambivalence. On the one hand, we want our children to go to school or to group care. It gives us some much-needed time away from them—time for ourselves or time to pursue our work. Sometimes parents have the normal feeling that they want to "get rid of" their children. They may secretly want to experience life as it was before they were parents. On the other hand, they love their children and wish to keep them near, to protect them, and to make sure all goes well with them. These ambivalent feelings are not always conscious and are often uncomfortable. When school begins, sometimes parents worry unduly about their children as a means of covering up, to themselves, their feelings of joy in their newfound freedom.

Parents may have other concerns as well. They may worry about the teacher's competence. The teacher is, after all, a stranger, and it is not easy to leave your child with a stranger. Why should a parent trust an unknown entity? Why should you believe that a teacher will take as good care of your daughter or son as you would?

Parents may also feel jealousy. "Suppose the teacher takes better care of Dolores than I do?" "What if Eddie loves the teacher more?"

Parents may further be concerned that they, as good parents, will be unmasked and judged by the teacher. "Suppose the teacher finds out that Paolo is not really the great creative genius that I believe he is?" What if the teacher discovers the child's flaws— that she is a thumbsucker, or wets the bed, or kicks and bites, or uses fresh language, or is disobedient? "Will the teacher see me as a bad parent when she discovers these traits in my child?"

Some of these parental feelings are understandable when they are examined in the light of your own history. You were once a child in school yourself. Perhaps you, like your own child, were shy or fearful about going to school for the first time. Parents also have feelings about teachers that are based on those past experiences. These feelings often resurface at school beginnings when parents recapture some of their own experiences with school entry and separation. Feelings of fear, anxiety, worry, and discomfort mixed with excitement are not unknown to parents as they enter a classroom with their children for the first time.

At a parents' meeting, a father said, "I felt good when George started in this center because he didn't have to worry about being late. When I was late, the teacher got angry. Here they don't worry about 'late.' "

An Informal Survey of Parents' Feelings

I sent a questionnaire to a group of forty-four parents whose children, aged ten months to four years, were in three different day-care centers. The parents were black, white, and Hispanic, male and female, and their socioeconomic status ranged from factory worker to college professor, from maintenance worker to doctor and lawyer. I asked them three questions:

What were your feelings when you knew that your child would soon be entering school or group care?

How did you feel the first day you accompanied your child to school or group care?

How did you feel about the separation from your child and your child's being in the teacher's care after the first few weeks had gone by?

Of the twenty-two who replied, many parents said they had mixed feelings when they knew their children would be entering group care. While they felt good because they knew, from friends or from experience, that the center was a safe and trustworthy place, they also felt worried about a variety of matters. Some worried about leaving their children. They wrote:

Was she too young at fourteen months? Would she become depressed or more clinging because of the separation?

My first feeling was that we were going to be apart for a couple of hours each day.

Sadness and loss that he was getting older and separating more from me.

How would she adapt being out of the closeness with me?

Some parents were concerned about their children's behavior:

Would she perform well?

I started thinking about how he would react when told to do something. How he would act when told to settle down the same time the other children do. My feelings are very deeply concerned with him being able to function correctly.

Some of the parents reported they were entirely positive about beginning group care for their children, but one commented, "Well, I wasn't happy because it was really the first time she would be away from me for a few hours a day, outside of her being with my family."

In describing their feelings when they actually accompanied their children to school, parents used words such as "nervous," "anxious," "sad," "worried," "apprehensive," "tense," and "strange." All the parents, except one, admitted to these emotions. Two said they thought they felt more nervous than their children did. Several stated that they felt it was a "loss," a "milestone," "a big change that she was starting to grow away from me." Several expressed very strong feelings:

It was very hard for me to leave, and I had tears in my eyes.

I also missed my child a lot. I felt anxious about what would happen in the new surroundings.

I didn't feel too good because I wasn't used to leaving my daughter with people I really didn't know.

Others expressed their worry about leaving a daughter or son with strangers. One parent wrote, "It's a little bit difficult for the parents because they are entrusting people they still don't know very well with what is most precious to them—their child."

Some parents made connections with their own experiences with separation. One wrote that she felt "Nervous. Excited. Apprehensive. Thrilled. It brought back fond memories of my first day of school—a day I had eagerly awaited for many months." Another felt "somewhat sad and tearful about leaving her this time and thinking about all the other partings in the future—and past, I'll bet."

One parent of a twenty-month-old recalled the third day:

[It] was probably the most traumatic for us both. I left the school after dropping him off. He cried miserably. I went home to clean the house in a torrent of tears and guilt for being a part of a society that uproot[s] babies from their mothers at such a young age. That afternoon, when I picked him up, he was listening intently to a story. We both cried and embraced after a long separation.

After the first few weeks had gone by, all the parents said they felt better. They used words such as "wonderful," "confident," "relieved," "secure," "positive," "comfortable," and "fine." These positive feelings built up because the separation was gradual and they saw that their children were happy. "She liked it, so I felt wonderful because the teachers treated her fine and she was happy with the other kids." "Yet in time," another wrote, "I learned that she just enjoyed it here very much. The teachers were supportive and wonderful to me as well as my child." Another summed up many of the other parents' feelings when she wrote, "As soon as a child shows signs of happiness, one feels relieved." Trust in the staff seemed to be at the core of parents' resolution of their anxious feelings.

> I felt that he was in good hands.

> I felt much better than I had anticipated. This was just another step but nothing anxious or worrisome. I trusted the staff.

Similar feelings and experiences were expressed by British parents of young children in four London preschools when I asked the same three questions.

Like the American parents, the British parents, anticipating their children's school entry, had varied feelings. Some were enthusiastic at the prospect of school beginning:

> I thought it would be very good for my daughter, that she would have lots of opportunities to learn to be a lot more independent . . . and . . . get used to being without Mum for some of the time.

> [I felt] GREAT, I knew that my daughter would enjoy it, and I needed the break.

Other parents were more ambivalent—they were both glad and sad:

I was pleased, but I was very anxious just in case he didn't like it.

I must be honest and say I hated the thought . . . I wanted my son to stay at home with me until he was five, but my husband said for his sake he should go. I wasn't being fair.

On the first day, most parents were worried, concerned, sad, "slightly emotional," and apprehensive. It seems that the actual initiation was very weighty for many mothers and fathers. They wrote with poignancy:

I felt a great sense of loss . . . but also a feeling of pride as I left her to mix with new friends and new teachers. I also felt as I left her, that she was no longer a baby, but the start of her growing up.

[I was] anxious at how he would cope. I felt that I would have liked to have stayed to "protect" him. Saying goodbye was harder for me than him, I think. All day I kept thinking "I wonder what he is doing now?" I was very pleased when he came out of school at the end of the first day, relieved that day one was over.

The British parents also found relief from worry through their trust and confidence in the staff.

I felt fine, because I knew that he was in safe hands.

Several parents on both sides of the Atlantic wrote about the support toward growth. "I still enjoy our times together," one parent said, "reading, playing, and experiencing new things, but we are both happier being able to grow in our separate ways."

Just because parents feel less worried after the separation has been tested and tried does not seem to mean that the initial feelings disappear entirely. One parent wrote, touchingly:

I still wonder if I've made the right choice. There are times during the day when I miss her very much. But it is a great comfort to me that she is so near where I work and I can readily go to see her and that she is in the care of such a wonderful staff. I think I would come to visit even more often, but the thought of coming and then leaving again sometimes deters me. As you can see, I'm not very good at partings.

Teachers' Feelings: Confidence and Nervousness

Teachers have many feelings about the start of school, too. Some are tremendously confident when school begins, excited at the prospect of meeting a new group of children. Others may be nervous and worry about what to do with children who may cry, or they may have concerns about how long their crying might last. Some teachers may feel uncomfortable being around many parents for several days and may wish to get them out of the room as soon as possible. Once the routines are established and children are comfortable, they may breathe a sigh of relief and feel that finally they can get down to the business of teaching.

There is nothing unusual about teachers feeling some

of the same worries and discomforts as the children and their parents. Just as you were once a child, in school, so were teachers. They have memories as you do, of their own school beginnings, some of which were positive and some probably not. These memories contribute to the feelings that are aroused as they become involved in first-day activities.

Teachers, like parents, have had personal experiences with several other forms of separation, such as graduation, vacations, changing jobs, moving, divorce, marriage, or death. How they were affected by any of these situations in the past may influence how they, and you, feel and behave when school begins.

A group of teachers, some of whom were also parents, participating in a workshop on separation, was asked to think of a word they associated with the word "separation." Here are some of their responses:

Fear
Anxiety
Pain
Alone
Angry
Venturing forth
Out of control
Rejection
Help
Distance
Unhappy

For almost all, "separation" conjured up a collection of feelings that were raw and unsettling. In discussing their responses, they explored the reasons for such unhappy associations. Their personal experiences with separation seemed to be the most potent molder of their present feelings—how their parents treated them when there was a separation. "I was told to be a big girl and not to cry. I was probably only four or five years old," one participant recalled.

They also saw past stressful events, such as the birth of a sibling or their own parents' absence from home for an extended period of time, as influences on their present feelings.

Some found that striking out on their own and venturing forth were gratifying separation experiences that led to intellectual expansion and new levels of self-confidence.

Perhaps if you examine your own feelings when school begins for your child, a connection to some of the emotions described here will be revealed. Once you are able to understand some of your own feelings, you may be more alert to similar feelings in your daughter or son.

Separation's Complex Impact

Separation affects children. It affects parents. It arouses feelings in teachers. School beginnings can be exciting as well as uncomfortable occasions. Along with those who are genuinely delighted that school is starting, there are frequently crying children or tense and nervous parents. Often teachers feel pulled by the conflicting needs of the children, the demands of the parents, and their own inclinations.

Where shall I put my son's sweater?

Could I have a few words with you privately about Melissa? She's a very sensitive child.

Where will the bus leave my daughter off?

Please don't let my son drink grape juice. It stains his clothes.

Mommy. I want my mommy. When's my mommy coming back?

By the end of the first day, the teacher's head may be spinning from the accumulated problems and concerns of the children and the parents, mixed with the excitement of a new group and a new year ahead. A situation that provokes so many feelings and so many memories is bound to produce reactions in all who are involved.

Chapter 2

GETTING TO THE ROOTS OF SEPARATION FEELINGS

Saying goodbye is an experience that occurs in all phases of human life and takes many forms. It starts at birth when the infant leaves the known, nine-month inner home for the strange outer world of bright lights, sounds, and the touch of human skin. It is seen in the wobbling of toddlers, practicing separation as they scoot away from parental beckoning. Preschoolers experience "goodbye" as they leave the security of home to enter an unknown world of school or center. School-age children mourn the loss of friends who move away. Separation characterizes many events in developing adult life—an adolescent breaks up with a girlfriend or boyfriend; a young adult graduates from college and charts a new course; adults move to a new home; a person changes jobs; someone gets married, another gets divorced; a spouse dies.

All these events are bound by a common thread. In each circumstance, an individual is leaving familiar territory and entering the unknown, the untried. A potential for growth and change exists in every separation experience, even though a temporary sense of

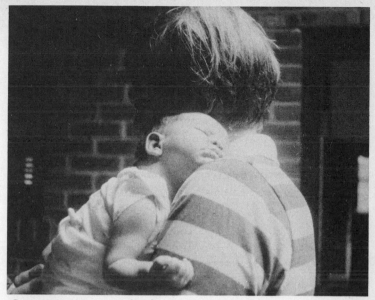

Separation starts at birth.

loss predominates. Few people set out on a new venture without thoughts of what they have left behind.

Sometimes ceremony lessens the impact of a loss by acknowledging a particular separation as a legitimate transition to a new phase of development. In some primitive cultures, rituals such as shaving a child's head may symbolize cutting him off from his past connections and indicate his entry into another stage of life. Spanking at a birthday party may be a modern counterpart of this custom. Other present-day events, such as debutante balls, graduations, baptisms, bar and bat mitzvahs, and weddings mark the transition from one stage of life to another.

School beginning is also a transition to a new stage for children as well as parents, but there is no unique ritual in our society that is culturally shared. A new lunch box, a pair of new shoes, a pencil case, or a new jacket or cap may be symbols to mark an event that is full of meaning and possibilities for children and parents. Yet there is no tradition that eases us through this important occasion like the one described by a mother who had lived on a kibbutz in Israel:

> The first-graders all took their belongings to their new classroom at the age of six. Parents, grandparents, and children attended a ceremony and everyone wore white shirts and there were speeches and songs. It was a real celebration, and it helped us all to realize that the first day of school was a very big change for adults, too.[1]

Attachment: The Roots of Separation Feelings

Many young children display strong reactions when they are separated, or even anticipate separation, from their parents—even if it is the briefest of partings. Where do the roots of these feelings lie?

There is some speculation that the roots are very deep. Two pediatricians, Marshall Klaus and John Kennell (1976) postulated the existence of a sensitive period immediately after birth in which babies and their parents were predisposed to bonding. Their research prompted them to conclude that this bonding was essential for later parent-child attachment and had far-reaching consequences. While these findings have aroused controversy and qualification, the idea that early and extended parent-infant contact is important has influenced hospitals to change maternity practices in an effort to be more humane. Whether or not early and extended contact affects the quality of attachment remains to be seen, but the fact that hospitals permit more parents and their newborns to remain together to strengthen the attachment process is noteworthy.

Though it may be an influential factor in development, this early bonding phenomenon, which involves parental feelings of concern and commitment toward the newborn infant, is qualitatively different from the stable, deep, and abiding attachment between parents and children that is usually formed during the first year of life. This is an enduring emotional tie that grows out of the day-to-day interactions between parents and children. This evolving attachment continues to be magnetic throughout the whole of life and has been defined as a tie that binds one person to another in space and endures over time.[2] Often this attachment prompts a parent to rush to the bedside of a sick child, though the "child" be an adult, the parent elderly, and the distance many miles.

The term "attachment" has special meaning. It is not the same as "dependence." Although the two terms are often used interchangeably, they are significantly different. Children who are securely attached to their parents have an abiding trust in their parents' reliability, which fosters their own burgeoning self-reliance and self-confidence.[3] Children who are dependent sidestep their own thrusts toward autonomy and lean on their parents instead. According to John Bowlby, the author of a major work about separation, dependence, which refers to an infant's state of helplessness, is present at its "maximum at birth and diminishes more or less steadily until maturity is reached, [whereas] attachment is altogether absent at birth and is not strongly in evidence until after an infant is past six months."[4] He further describes dependency in human relations as a condition to be avoided and attachment as a condition to be cherished.

Frequently, young children, who tightly hold their parent's body or hide in their clothing when entering an unfamiliar setting, such as school or another's home, are often regarded as dependent rather than as attached. However, such actions are legitimate, inborn attachment behaviors that keep infants and young children close to their parents. Clinging, crying, calling, or following are characteristic of all young humans and are explained by ethologists (those who study the connections between human and animal life) as remnants of an urgent, primitive protective mechanism.

Attachment relationships are not only defined by clinging or crying. Many are embroidered with smiles and joyous exchanges when parents and children strike a comfortable balance with one another. These chil-

Many attachment relationships are characterized by trust.

dren seem to have an intuitive understanding of and faith in their parents' predictability. They seem to know each other well, enjoy each others' company, and trust one another's behavior.

How Attachment Develops

Although there are speculations that bonding may begin immediately after birth, a wide variety of experiences must occur between infants and their parents before attachment becomes secure.

A baby may "belong" to you, the parent, in your view, long before you truly "belong" to the baby. Dr. Margaret Mahler, who did research about babies and their mothers, evolved a theory about the development of young children's sense of self.[5] She believes that for the first two or three months babies experience parents as extensions of themselves, unable to completely distinguish the boundaries that exist between them.

A young baby is described as believing that the nipple containing milk appears in her mouth by magic, called up by her own desires to relieve her hunger pangs. If an infant could talk she might say, "Oh, I'm so hungry. What I need is some milk. Ah, here's the nipple with milk. How powerful I am to make it come to me when I need it." Mahler defines this as babies' sense of their own omnipotence.

Her theory states that at around four or five months of age a "hatching" takes place as babies begin to break out of the psychological shell that wrapped them and their parents together. Little by little they begin to perceive the difference between themselves and their parents, and to know the parents' bodies as different from their own, the parents' faces as different from other faces. They begin to know and to prefer the parents.

Currently, there are challenges to this theory by those who see the infant's awareness of self at an earlier age.[6] Recent research indicates that babies as neonates of only a few days old may be able to distinguish their mothers from others.[7]

Usually, by the middle of the first year, through intimate looking, touching, hearing, speaking, seeing, and by means of their own development, babies have become attached to their parents.[8] They come to know that the parents are their own particular persons, whose looks, smell, touch, and sound are special. This attachment is a basis of human relatedness from which children derive the capacity for strong feelings about important people. It is this attachment that enables children to become friends and lovers, as well as enemies.

As infants grow and develop, their attachment to their parents becomes more complex, more laden with feelings and meanings for all involved. Evidence of the strength of this bond is seen at around eight or nine months of age, when babies often recoil, hide their faces, or sometimes shriek at the sight of a stranger. It is as if the baby were saying to the stranger, "I really know the person whom I love best—and it's not you." This occurrence is often called "stranger anxiety." As a child continues to develop, aided by his secure, certain relationship with his parents, this intense reaction to strangers usually begins to fade.

In fact, toddlers between ten and fifteen or sixteen months of age tend to be the very opposite of suspicious seven to nine-month olds. They are like joyous world explorers, especially in the company of their parents. They have been described as having a "love affair with the world."[9] When not in the company of their parents, toddlers of this age often seem in low-key moods. They seem to be most free to explore when they have a secure base from which to roam. Mahler refers to toddlers of this age as "practicing."[10] In practicing their newly acquired walking skills, they behave, and often look, as if they were intoxicated. They freely wander off to see new and thrilling sights that have opened up to them, now that they are upright.

With this tremendous new scope to their lives also comes a particular danger, according to Mahler's theory. Their separateness from their parents is now a physical reality. They realize that they are vulnerable, that they still need care and protection. This realization often drives them back to the arms, laps, or legs of their parents for "emotional refueling."[11] It is often as bewildering to parents as it is to the caregivers of toddlers between eighteen and twenty-two or twenty-four months of age that such formerly "independent" beings could become so clingy. This period, which Mahler calls the "rapprochement crisis," is frequently one of the most difficult periods for parents as well as teachers,[12] because, as Resch puts it, "all hell breaks loose" when children are left in group care or even at home with babysitters.

Not only are most children this age painfully aware of their need for their "attachment person," but they are still developing the cognitive, as well as the emotional, ability to deal with that person's absence. While many children are able to call up in their mind's eye a mental image of that person by the time they are eighteen or twenty months old, that ability is not always reliable. This internal picture develops out of the pleasurable as well as the not-so-pleasurable experiences that the baby has, from birth on, with the prime caregiver. The stability of that image is highly influenced by the toddler's emotions. Under tense, stressful conditions the mental image is often harder to maintain than in relaxed, comfortable times. For toddlers, out of sight is often out of mind, and parental absence is very hard to bear. It may seem to these young children that the beloved, missed adult will never return. Prolonged crying, intense rage, and uncontrollable sobbing are common in eighteen- to twenty-four-month-old toddlers. It is not surprising that parents—and just as frequently teachers and caregivers—often feel incompetent, frustrated, or even angry at children in these circumstances.

When a toddler becomes a two-year-old, the intensity of these attachment feelings continues to be aroused when separation occurs, or is even suspected by a child. For a child of twenty to twenty-four or twenty-six months, separation can be especially difficult. By this age, children have attached significance and strong feelings to the departure of parents, and they often become inconsolable at separations, even those of short duration.[13] Two-year-old children have a profound understanding of your very special importance to them. They know, deeply, their own tremendous need for and reliance on you. This knowledge increases their terror and panic when you leave them.

Translated into the language of a child, those feelings might be stated like this:

> I really know that you are my parent. I know that I need you to take care of me in all situations. I am afraid that if you leave me, I won't be able to take care of myself. It makes me angry that you want to go away like that, and I feel sad and hurt. So, in order not to feel that way, I'm going to do what I know how to do best to keep you here. I can cry. I can hold on to you. I can follow you. I can call you. These things ought to work, because they've worked before.

About Separating

As children grow into preschoolers of three and four, their separation reactions take a different form from those they had at age one or two. For one thing, most children have completed the phase of their "second" or "psychological" birth.[14] They have emerged from infancy and toddlerhood with a clearer sense of themselves as individuals, attached to, but distinctly separate from you the parents. They are described as having attained a state of "constancy," which is "the enduring inner conviction of being me and nobody else."[15]

Another reason that three- and four-year-olds may react to separation differently from two-year-olds and toddlers is that they are able to consistently mentally represent their absent parents. As any adult knows, there is some comfort in being able to conjure up in your thoughts the person you are missing. Out of sight is no longer out of mind.

Eventually, the ability to separate is a necessity if children are to develop as autonomous and self-reliant beings. It is a capacity that most parents try to support. It is built up in preschool children through the cumulative separation experiences they have had, such as staying with friends, grandparents, and caregivers, and going to birthday parties or visiting in other children's homes. The way in which you and your child behave and feel when you say goodbye will influence the many goodbyes that inevitably lie ahead.

Both of you contribute to the emotional climate of any leave-taking situation. Some children find parting easy—others find it difficult. Some can say goodbye with feeling, and then make a quick recovery. Others have less tolerance for separation, are deeply affected and unable to pull themselves back together emotionally without adult encouragement and support. Adults are no different—some say goodbye with aplomb, others with weight and pain. What distinguishes adult reactions from those of children is that we adults have a longer history of saying goodbyes than our children and we understand the meaning of time. How we as adults have experienced separations in our lives up to this point dictates in great measure whether we are weepers, stoics, or copers and whether separation has come to mean a temporary loss or abandonment.

And So to School

Being able to separate comfortably, becoming a "real school person" at three, four, and five is most gratifying and pleasurable for many young children. Often preschoolers who are starting school for the first time are excited by the new environment replete with attractive playthings and a bevy of children their own age. Separation for these children is an adventure and a challenge.

However, the ability to tolerate the stress of separation and the ability to adjust to strange and new situations varies greatly from child to child. Not all three-, four-, or even five-year-olds are able to enter school with complete comfort.

Certain developmental abilities are needed. They have been cited by Anna Freud (1965) as necessary to a preschooler's competent entry to nursery school. She states that self-feeding and control of bowel and bladder are prerequisites because they indicate growing bodily independence. The ability to relate to other children and to accept them as partners in their own right, plus the ability to use play materials in self-initiated and directed activities, are further indications that young children of three to five are ready to enter nursery school. Freud also states that impulse control and the ability, at some times, to wait a turn, tolerate frustration, and express negative feelings appropriately are also necessary to insure a child's successful entry into preschool.

We know many children who, on entering school, fit these guidelines and are able to leave their parents with a minimum of stress. We also know that there are other children who do not entirely fit this description and for whom entry and continued presence in the nursery school or day-care center is stressful and unsuccessful.

Because these guidelines do not apply to children under three, a more prolonged and gradual separation period is required for children of this age. Since they have not yet developed the coping skills seen in preschoolers such as language and the understanding of time, infants and toddlers need maximum support from parents and teachers when they enter group care.

Since parents are largely the mediators of their young children's experiences, they help children understand the meaning of events and of other people's behavior through the way they explain these to children and the way that they, the parents, behave. Parents translate separation at school entry in many different ways and communicate a variety of ideas and feelings about the event to their children. Because these ideas and feelings are expressed through the attachment relationship, these partings are laden with feelings. Some parents and children say goodbye with ease and comfort, while others find it a strain. All of us bring to the separation a bit of our past and we may reenact, through our actions and feelings, our own experience of going to school for the first time. And although we all desperately long to protect our children forever, "we still must let them go. Hoping we have equipped them for the journey. Hoping they will wear their boots in the snow. Hoping when they fall down, they can get up again. Hoping."[16]

Yet here at school entry lies a wonderful opportunity for parents to contribute to their children's learning and to enhance their self-confidence through separations that are well achieved. Children who are supported by their parents and their teachers as they separate from home have the opportunity to move fearlessly into new realms of learning and growth.

Chapter
3

UNDERSTANDING YOUR CHILD'S GOODBYE BEHAVIOR

Children communicate with us through their eyes, the quality of their voices, their body postures, their gestures, their mannerisms, their smiles, their jumping up and down, their listlessness. They show us, by the way they do things as well as by what they do, what is going on inside them. When we have come to see children's behavior through the eyes of its meaning to them, from inside out, we shall be well on our way to understanding them.[1]

What are some of the clues children give us about their feelings connected with leaving home and entering school? For children, "leaving home" is often a more powerful experience than "entering school." Separation events usually involve a slipping back or a giving up in order to then step forward. When learning to walk, children eventually give up crawling. When graduating from high school, adolescents give up the security of known teachers and friends to go forth to college or into the work world. When leaving nursery school for kindergarten, children leave a familiar setting. There is little growth without some pain or anxiety. As we step forward to a new level or challenge, we necessarily leave something behind. Without these dips and rises, life would be flat, and people would be undeveloped. Yet the younger the individual, the more help he or she needs in moving forward without wounds. Children tell us through their behavior that they need our help, that their feelings are too overwhelming to manage alone.

Very Good Behavior

Sometimes children are very good in school. No one can tell they are hurting inside. They keep to themselves. They never get into trouble. Teachers often overlook them in the midst of the swirling life of the classroom. Such a child was Kelly.

Kelly was a four-year-old boy. His face often wore a blank expression. He rarely smiled. He never cried. He spoke very little. When the group had a music and singing time, Kelly stood at the edge of the seated group, watching. When the group sat together for a snack, Kelly sat, but refused to eat. When his mother brought him to school, and when she came to pick him up, he was compliant and obedient. He never made a fuss. Kelly hardly played with any of the equipment. If he painted, it was a lackadaisical three or four strokes of the brush and he was done. He seldom spoke to other children and only spoke to the teacher when asked a direct question. He spoke in short phrases or single words.

When, by November, Kelly's behavior had not changed, the teacher became concerned. Since this was a cooperative nursery school, mothers periodically helped in the room. When Kelly's mother came to help, the teacher noticed a dramatic difference in Kelly's behavior. He was talkative, he ate lustily, he used the equipment, and seemed to get pleasure in his play.

The teacher arranged a conference with the mother to discuss her concern for the vast difference in Kelly's behavior with and without his mother. They came to the joint conclusion that perhaps Kelly was missing his mother. It seemed to the teacher that while Kelly was physically in school, he remained mentally at home.

Together, they made plans as if Kelly were again starting school from the first day. His mother began to stay in the room with him for about one hour each day. She talked with him about missing her. They played together. They planned for her to stay each day that week until snack time. After the first week, Kelly and his mother decided together that she would stay once a week. She did so for a month.

At the same time his mother was in the room, Kelly began to relate to the assistant teacher, staying close to her, speaking softly to her. She discovered that if she sat next to him at snack time, he would wait until all the children had left the table and then would eat. He still refused to participate in music time, so the assistant sat next to him, while he stood watching the group. She read to him, led him to the table, and encouraged him to play with Play-Doh while she sat next to him. He began to talk more, to both children and adults. He began to use the play equipment. His body relaxed and his face began to exhibit more varied expressions. By March he had begun to eat when the others ate. By

Sometimes children sit at the edge of an activity until they feel comfortable in school.

April he began to make a friend and after spring vacation, he sat near the music group. One day, with the assistant's hand holding his, he took a turn walking around in a circle to the music, wearing his cowboy hat.

He had finally come to school.

It was fortunate that Kelly's teacher recognized his lack of involvement in school activities as a separation reaction, even though it wasn't until November. By allowing him the time he needed to coalesce his home self with his school self, his teacher and his mother, working together, helped him to grow in competence and in self-confidence.

It was also fortunate that his mother was a nurse and that her working hours permitted her to be with Kelly when he came to school in the morning. Another parent, with more conventional working hours, might have been able to stay at the end of the school day, or arrange to come for lunch. Perhaps phoning at strategic times might have helped.

Sometimes, however, children are not at all ready to enter school or group life. If, for example, Kelly had not made a relationship first with the assistant teacher and then with the children, if he had not started to play, if his body and facial expressions had not relaxed, if he had not started to eat in school, then he might have been saying that he was not ready to leave home, not ready to come to school. While such situations do not happen frequently, they do occur. You need to be aware of such a possibility and to be alert to your child's behavior. If there is a vast difference between your son or daughter's behavior at home and that at school, discuss this with the teacher. Try to work out an appropriate plan with the teacher that increases your child's comfort—and yours. Beginning school is not an endurance contest.

Delayed Reaction

Often children do not send out the strong cues that Kelly did. They may come to school bright and bouncy, delighted to be there, excited to play, full of fun and pleasure.

Three-year-old Tania cheerfully kissed her mother goodbye every morning. She painted with enthusiasm, used many colors, and seemed to enjoy her activity. She used dough and water with pleasure and found companionship in the dress-up area. She loved music and books and puzzles. She was a happy-go-lucky girl.

One day, three weeks after school began, she threw herself on the floor, crying hysterically for her mother. She was inconsolable. The teacher phoned her mother that evening to ask if anything unusual had happened. The mother could think of nothing. After all, she recalled, the move to this present new home had taken place several months before.

After that, Tania cried repeatedly when her mother brought her to the center. Together the teacher and the mother decided to see if it would help if the mother stayed a little longer each morning rather than leaving right away. It took several months of this maternal support before Tania felt safe. Even so, Tania occasionally cried for her mother and refused to play.

The move to the new home seemed to be a bigger event in the life of the small girl than anyone had realized. It had taken many months for the child to internalize that experience. It was not until she had been in the center for a few weeks that she was able to express her great distress. Two separations, one from her old home and one from her mother, were more than she could bear.

Children do not have the experience with loss that adults have. They do not know that there are boundaries to these experiences. Children often feel that the loss will never end, that they will never stop feeling sad, that they will never stop crying. They need help to understand that life is not all like this and that the lonely, sad times have ends as well as beginnings. Tania's mother and her teacher, working together toward a common goal—Tania's comfort and ability to control her life—helped her to grow toward the belief that she was a strong person who could overcome hard-to-bear feelings. Tania also learned that though these feelings continued to overwhelm her at

The parent can be seen sitting nearby. The distance between parent and child is distinct yet minimal, fostering the boy's developing capacity for trust.

times, she could count on comfort and support from her mother at home and from her teacher at school.

Regressive Behaviors: Thumb Sucking, Eating, Wetting, Sleeping

Tania regressed in her behavior, slipping back to a stage of development reminiscent of toddlerhood. Rex Speers, a psychoanalyst, found that children entering nursery school normally repeat phases of their earlier development.[2] He believes that this repetition is desirable for children's successful adaptation to school. As they behave in ways that echo their past, Speers says, children make use of their mothers' presence in the classroom to gain self-assurance. Such normal regressions occur when children cry, complain, plead to be taken home, refuse to play, and cling tenaciously to their mothers.

Sometimes children need to fall back a few steps in order to then move ahead. Perhaps you have noticed that tendency in yourself or in other adults. I once knew a writer who, before she could sit down to the serious business of writing, spent half an hour sharp-

In entering nursery school children may interact with their parents as they did when they were toddlers.

ening every pencil in the house. It was a bit of regressive behavior that seemed to provide the needed energy for the task before her.

One of the most obvious remnants of much younger behavior in preschoolers is thumb sucking. Some children who have given it up may, with the onset of school or day care, begin again, only to give it up once more after they have become comfortable in the new setting. Others who still need to suck their thumbs might be seen sucking more frequently both at home and at school, especially when the parent leaves or when they eat or sleep. It is not uncommon to see children increase their thumb sucking at the end of the day, when they are tired. Some children might also want to return to the comfort of a bottle, even though they have stopped using one. They might ask to bring their bottles to school to use for comfort in times of stress.

Do you feel uncomfortable seeing the return of these behaviors? Perhaps you thought you had seen their end. Maybe you worry that once they have returned, the thumb sucking or the need for the bottle will never stop. It is highly unlikely that this will occur, however. Children behave in certain ways because of some specific need. Once their need for feeling secure is met—through the teacher's help and your support—children will probably abandon the regressive behavior.

Observe your child at home to see just when the increased or revived thumb sucking takes place. Perhaps it is when there's "nothing to do," or when you are busy with chores or preoccupied with your own concerns. Your most helpful response is to ignore, yet accept, the behavior. The more you say "Take your thumb out of your mouth," the more children seem to cling to it. Telling adults, "Take that cigarette out of your mouth," often produces the same results. Offering an interesting activity, such as helping to scrape the carrots, or scrub the potatoes, or set the table is usually a welcome relief to a boy or girl.

Another regressive behavior related to sucking is seen in eating. The three-year-old in the following anecdote becomes troubled about his snack at the center.

> Although Sean was busy with blocks, he noticed the teacher handling grapes for snack. He stood up quickly, dropping the blocks, and cried softly as he rushed over to the teacher, saying, "No, I don't want this, I only want crackers for snack." He spoke quickly, with much feeling.
>
> "Come and look at the food, Sean," said the teacher gently. "These are grapes, and this is cheese. You don't have to eat them, but just come closer and look."
>
> "I don't have to eat them," he whimpered.

Children often display feelings of stress at snack or lunch time in school. They may eat too little or too much. Food is frequently a tangible reminder of home, and teachers sometimes see young children act in a worried manner about eating. You may see changes in children's appetites at home as well around the time of school beginning. Think of how your own appetite is affected when you're about to have a job interview or you've got a big project to do, or you are very worried about the well-being of someone close to you.

Regression is sometimes seen in children's physical movements. In a study by Curry & Tittnich, children who were "graceful and skillful in performing motor feats" at school entry "suddenly [became] quite

Enjoyment of eating is often a good sign of comfort.

clumsy, tripping over nothing at all and causing all sorts of accidents to [themselves] and others."[3]

Ellie was swaggering in large circles around the room attending to the children and their activity rather than where she was walking. She focused on the children to the front, side, or back but not on those directly next to her. As a result she tripped and fell three times over children and toys that were in her path. As she fell, she glanced at the obstacle, then immediately regained her farsighted vision. Her movements were quick as she scrambled to her feet, arms straight, with the palms of her hands flat on the floor to balance herself, as a toddler might.

Toilet accidents and sleep disturbances, especially among two-and-a-half- and three-year-olds and sometimes even among four- and five-year-olds, are generally common in stressful situations. These regressions of well-learned skills frequently happen around the time children begin school. You may see bed wetting, constipation, stomachaches, or wet underpants and clothing. Children may resist going to sleep at school as well as at home. Nap or rest time at the center may find children fidgety, squirming, tense, or unable to stop talking or giggling. Children may wake in the middle of the night; they may have nightmares, or refuse, as they never did before, to go to bed. The opposite may also occur—children who never napped may begin to do so or regular nappers may take very long, extended two- or three-hour naps.

How many adults, faced with a trip across the country or abroad, moving to a new home, going to college, or starting a new job, find themselves plagued with constipation, diarrhea, loss of appetite, overeating, or sleeplessness? Our bodies often express our feelings, even if we are not aware of them.

Nicholas, twenty-six months old, took a daily afternoon nap at home. When he started day care, he refused to sleep. No amount of rocking, back rubbing, singing, or vocal soothing would induce him to sleep. Finally the caregiver stopped trying to give him a nap and allowed him to play after lunch instead. Often he fell asleep on a soft chair or couch. After a few weeks of this he allowed the caregiver to put him on a cot in the nap room.

Why might young children be so worried about sleeping at school or day care or at home? In falling asleep, children give up whatever small amount of control they have over themselves when they are awake. Giving up that control, for some children, is not easily done. It is especially difficult at a time when they are worried about where their parents are and whether or not their parents will know where to find them. Some children think that if they are not sure where their parents are, then their parents may not be sure where they, their children, are. Some of these concerns may remain with your child when she comes home at the end of the day. Reassuring her, when she wakes up or goes to sleep, that you are there to take care of her will be a comfort. Do not expect the problem to go way instantly. These feelings take time to be resolved.

While regressions in motor control, eating, toileting, sleeping, and sucking are frequently associated with separation reactions, they are also commonly seen whenever children feel stress, either at home or at school.

You can help your child during stressful times by recognizing his or her feelings. "You don't seem to be very hungry tonight. I wonder if something is bothering you?" Even if your son or daughter is not able to say what the trouble is—and many young children cannot—your understanding attitude will help.

You can also help your child by listening to what he or she says about missing you or about angry feelings. Often young children speak about their anger in very graphic, violent-sounding terms. One mother, nightly, heard her four-year-old son sing a "song" he made up:

He will just do nothing at all,
He will just sit there in the noonday sun.
And when they speak to him, he will not answer them

Because he does not care to.
He will stick them with spears and put them in the garbage.
When they tell him to eat his dinner, he will just laugh at them,
And he will not take his nap, because he does not care to.
He will not talk to them, he will not say nothing.
He will just sit there in the noonday sun.
He will go away and play with Panda.
He will not speak to nobody because he doesn't have to.
And when they come to look for him they will not find him
Because he will not be there.
He will put spikes in their eyes and put them in the garbage,
And put the cover on.
He will not go out in the fresh air or eat his vegetables.
Or make wee-wee for them, and he will get as thin as a marble.
He will not do nothing at all.
He will just sit there in the noonday sun.[4]

Sometimes children may talk about the teacher negatively when school first begins. This may be children's way of disguising how angry they really are at their parents—it is much safer to be angry at a relative stranger. However, if you feel that there is some legitimate concern about the teacher, it is your responsibility to visit the school informally. Good schools will be hospitable to a parent's visit.

Looking and Talking

Often children show through looking and talking that they are not yet able to rely on a mental image of their parent as a source of comfort and reassurance when that parent is not present. They require an extra dose of parental and teacher help.

Two-and-a-half-year-old Christopher needed his grandmother to sit in the room with him for more than a week before she was able to move to a small library room connected to the classroom. Christopher often walked into the room and circled around her. When he was in the classroom, he frequently looked in through the open door, checking to see if she were still there.

A child's internal picture comes from repeated interactions and experiences with the loved person. The ability to hold this image develops slowly and in toddlers is unstable when the person is away. Christopher used his eyes as well as language as techniques to maintain his grandmother's image.

"I will not cry," he said. "No, I will not cry. Nana will not go? No, Nana will not go. She will be in the library. She will not leave Christopher. Christopher will go to school. Nana will wait in the library."

Despite the grandmother's repeated reassurances that she would wait in the library, he asked the same questions again and again.

Children's use of language may provide other clues to their feelings about separation. Refusal to talk, reversion to baby talk, or excessive talking may be signals that a child is worried.

Four-year-old-Shawnique never spoke a word to the teacher during the entire year. She spoke only occasionally to other children, although she played frequently with them. She painted, used clay, listened to stories, and sat on the teacher's lap, but refused to speak to her despite the teacher's most creative efforts. Her mother said that she never stopped talking at home.

This girl's refusal to speak possibly indicated her incomplete separation adaptation. Perhaps it was her way of leaving a part of herself at home. Bringing objects from home or keeping a photograph of her family in her cubby might have helped to bridge the gap. Possibly a visit to the home by her teacher might have made a stronger link of the two worlds for this child.

While some children may display anxiety through silence or continual talk, others may use language to master their feelings. Parents' and teachers' words, too, can help, even with the youngest children. However, "Mom will be back as soon as we've had lunch" is reassuring only if it is true.

Sometimes children use words to reassure themselves, as if the words themselves had a physical presence.

Every morning, Miriam looked at her mother and questioned, "Are you going to work? At the hospital?" "Yes," her mother replied while kissing and hugging her. "Bye bye! Have a nice time today."

Miriam took the teacher's proffered hand, saying,

"My mommy is going to work. To the hospital. I'll stay in school. She'll come back to get me, right?" The teacher reassured her that her mother would be back after work. Miriam went to paint at the easel.

Through their language, children have the ability to let adults know that they need help.

Arthur, in the midst of snack time, begins to sob. "I want my mommy!" Three other children watch him intently. The teacher hugs him and says, "I guess you're missing your mommy. She'll be coming back soon." He stops crying and reorganizes himself. The other children seem visibly relieved.

Children's language also offers opportunities for parents to take some appropriate action.

All the way to the center, Sarah tells her mother not to go to work. "You can stay in school and help the teacher," she suggests to her mother.
"I know you miss me, Sarah, and when I'm at work I miss you, too. So I will call you on the phone when I get to work today and have a little chat with you. Let's tell your teacher about this plan so that she'll be prepared for my call."

Coping with separation may take the form of using baby talk instead of more mature language. You can help your child by acknowledging this regression as a normal step in growing up. Admonishing a girl or boy to speak in a normal manner may make him or her feel ashamed. The following anecdote, from a teacher's diary, describes how he uses a music time for responding to baby talk in his four-year-old group.

As the group settled down for music, I noticed Eleanor and Amy engaged in "Ga Ga" talk. I saw a dazzling array of different feelings expressed through playful body language and cooing tones. I had the feeling that they were completely themselves. Vanished for the moment were the pretenses and obfuscations of feelings so often accompanying the use of proper language.

Sensing the moment ripe for baby movement, I asked, "Show me how you move like a baby." Silence. Shocked, blank faces. The children momentarily became stupefied when confronted with the reality of acting out some of their repressed fantasies.

Finally, after a long silence, Adam volunteered. He is strong, secure, and playfully rebellious—far removed from a helpless "baby self." He was in a position to venture into the "baby" role and have fun with it.

And what fun he had! Getting on hands and knees, he playfully crawled, rolled, and scampered around the floor. All the while he made playful, realistic baby sounds. Soon all the others followed.[5]

Increased Dependence

Teachers often see otherwise competent children become increasingly dependent during the first weeks of school or day care. They refuse to dress themselves or protest that they cannot, demand help in the simplest of tasks, refuse to pour their own juice or milk, need the teacher's lap many times during the day, and cling to, follow, or shadow the adults in the classroom. Their behaviors seem to say, "I am feeling very little and not up to my usual competent self. Give me just a little extra babying for a short period of time and it will provide the fuel I need so that I can get up and go on my own steam."

You may see similar behaviors at home. Les wants to be dressed in the morning; Jason refuses to be dressed. Camillo constantly crawls into his mother's lap; Annie follows her mother from room to room, crying if she goes out of view. You will begin to know that these may be starting-school behaviors. They are, for the most part, temporary, and will probably disappear as the children are reassured that you have sent them to school or day care to have a good, happy time and that the teachers can take care of them. Trust of this sort takes time to develop.

You may notice that many behaviors associated with eating, sleeping, competence, language, and toileting are exhibited again by children when they return to school after an illness or an extended absence, or if something unusual or upsetting has occurred at home. A lost pet, a car accident, a robbery, a weekend away from home, a parent away on a trip are all incidents that might trigger a change in a child's behavior when she goes to school.

Security Objects

Remember Linus and his blanket in the *Peanuts* cartoon? We laugh at Linus because our own children, or our friends' children, drag around shreds of blankets, tattered and rubbed-out stuffed animals, old diapers, or other "cozies," and often need to take them to school or other out-of-home places. Perhaps you remember having such a security object yourself. Somehow these things seem to make children feel

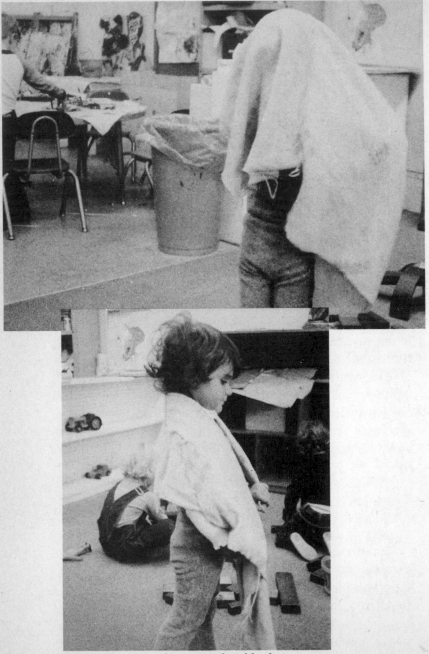

Where she goes, there goes her blanket.

good, as though they carry a bit of home with them wherever they go.

Children seem to grant security objects special qualities and endow them with important powers. Just watch what happens when a boy or girl misplaces the object! A well-known psychiatrist, D.W. Winnicott, calls these "transitional objects." He explains: "It is not the object itself, of course, that is transitional; it represents the infant's transition from a state of being merged with the mother to a state of being in relation to the mother as something outside and separate."[6]

The teddy bear or blanket supports a child's journey to growing up from infancy to early childhood. This journey leads them away from being part of the parent toward being persons separate from the parent. Because these objects have such significance for young children, they seem to provide a sense of security when children move from the familiarity of the home to the unfamiliarity of the school or center or other new places. The objects children bring from home are often more important at first than the activities to which they are drawn in school:

Ilana worked with pegs and puzzles while holding on to a ring that was far too large for her to wear on her finger. She would not let go of it even though it made using the manipulative toys she was working with more difficult.[7]

Sometimes children use things from the classroom itself as transitional objects in an effort to master their separation feelings. You may see your own child doing something like this:

Daniella strode over to the dress-up shelf. She began to throw clothes and shoes haphazardly over her shoulder, tossing them into the air, until she found her favorite black derby hat. She popped it on her head. A large grin immediately appeared on her face.

Several times during the day she was seen looking at herself in the mirror while wearing the derby. For months she frequently wore it all morning, even putting it under her cot when she took a nap.

Children also turn to their security objects at other times of heightened stress. Before you decide that it *must* be a separation reaction you are seeing as Michael clings to his blanket or Sandra mouths her stuffed bunny, consider all the possible causes—those related to school, such as inappropriate expectations, a lack of interesting activities, children's unchecked aggression, crowding, a teacher who yells; and those related to home life, such as tension or discord, lack of sleep, too many visitors.

Relations with Other Children

Through their uncomfortable relations with other children and with adults in school or other forms of child care, young children often show that separation is more stressful than they can handle. This may take the form of belligerence or withdrawal. Do not assume that all angry behavior is connected to separation reactions, however.

The same Christopher who worried and clung to his grandmother in the library also provoked others and disobeyed the teacher.

Christopher saw a plastic cauliflower that Joshua had dropped on the floor. When Christopher grabbed it, Joshua, astonished, said, "Hey, that's mine!" Angrily, Christopher threw it in Joshua's face. Joshua yelled, "I don't like that!" and glared at Christopher, who opened his eyes wide, laughed mischievously, and ran off in circles all around the room.

When the teacher told Christopher to pick up the cauliflower and to talk to Joshua about it, Christopher ran to the bookshelf and sat down to look at a book.

Why would children who are feeling worried about separation hit others, be disobedient, or destroy things in the classroom or at home? Consider this: One way to get rid of scary feelings is to fight them by taking very active steps. Throwing things, hitting, or arguing with others gives one the illusion of tremendous activity. It is as if children feel that they must do something to make themselves feel less worried. They are less concerned with the consequences of their antisocial behavior than they are with eliminating the fear they feel.

Sometimes children behave in a frantic manner in school:

Adam . . . flitted around from one thing to another . . . When the teacher tried to get him to [complete] a drawing, he told her . . . "I can't— you do it!" He treated the guinea pig like an inanimate object . . . he ran around the room as if he expected to be chased.

He did not pay any attention to his mother . . . when she left. But when a girl spoke to her father on the play phone, he grabbed the phone out of her hand and said, "When are you coming back?" On a number of occasions he ran in the opposite direction when he was told that it was time to go home and that his mother was waiting for him. Although he seemed almost desperate to make contact with children, he went about it by repeating what they said, grabbing things from them, taking over what they were doing, and trying to create excitement by getting silly with them.[8]

You may see behavior similar to this at home. Although your first impulse may be to stop the activity or use a heavy-handed attitude, try to use another tactic. It is calm reassurance that the child needs—reassurance that you will always return and reassurance that you understand how worried he feels. It may take a bit of time—days or weeks—for the child to return to more balanced behavior.

Coping Through Play

It is perhaps through play that children find their most satisfactory means of coming to terms with and mastering their reactions to separation. Developing intellectual skills is necessary for children to understand separation.[9] Before age three, a child begins to attach meaning and feelings to a parent's departure. To the extent that he can use a caregiver's presence, and eventually language and play to find relief from sad and angry feelings, he shows his potential for growth.

Three-year-old Marina throws her doll out of her room every morning before going to school. She tells her mother, "I don't want to go to school." Her mother acknowledges this by saying, "I know you don't want to go." Then she helps Marina dress, gives her breakfast, and takes her to school. Marina initiates a hide-and-seek game with the teacher when she arrives. This goes on for several months.

What can we say about Marina? Is this a problem or is this a child at work, coping with leaving home and going to school? Marina is using symbolic play to aid her adjustment to this new experience. She is practicing control over her own life. It is she who throws the doll out of the room, unlike the real situation in which she is taken to school. In playing hide-and-seek, it is she who has the control, unlike the real situation. In the real situation she has no control, for it is her mother who decides to take her to school.

As adults, we attempt to manage our feelings and behavior when events occur over which we have little control. It is when we lose control, when we are unable to rally ourselves to take action, that we feel unsatisfied with ourselves and defeated. Children feel the same way.

Role playing is an important and self-initiated activity that serves a multitude of functions. Through roles, children try out various ways of "being." Taking on the role of the one who offers nurturing may be one way a child can be both nurtured as well as nurturing. In tending to a doll, a girl or boy may be caring for the doll as if the doll were him or herself. In the following anecdote of two three-year-old boys, the roles of baby and mother are clearly enacted, allowing both children to feel cared for as well as caring.

Andrew is the "mother." At his feet is a wicker laundry basket with Nathan sitting in it. He is the "baby." Andrew gives Nathan an affectionate look

The child feels nurtured as well as nurturing.

and asks, "Do you want more?" The "baby" replies in a high, squeaky voice, "Yes." Andrew carefully places himself down into the basket, half resting on the edge. His chest is about on eye level with the "baby." He sticks his chest out, offering his "breast" to the "baby." The "baby" pretends to suck through Andrew's shirt. Andrew wraps his left arm snugly around the "baby's" neck. He has a very serious look on his face.

Pretend play of this sort may help children feel more confident about their parents' continuing nurturance even when they are not present. Witnessing such an intimate scene may cause some adults discomfort. However, it is natural for very young boys to "try out" feminine, as well as masculine, activities in their play. It is also a boy's way of practicing a nurturing role.

Make-believe is a rich resource of healing for preschool children. You may see children soothing their own feelings as you observe them at play. You may see them attempting to gain control, as in "fighting fires."

Gerald was riding a trike and making sirenlike sounds. He abruptly jumped off the trike and ran around, yelling, "Fire! Fire! Quick, there's a fire over there. Get the fire hats, hurry!" He pulled on an imaginary hat and rushed back toward his parked trike, shouting "Hurry! The fire! We need to put out the fire! C'mon! Fire! Fire!"

Perhaps the dangerous fire was a symbol for things that often raged out of control in Gerald's small life. Play is one way a child can practice being in charge.

As children begin to adapt to school and to the temporary loss of a parent, they begin to demonstrate their tolerance for "the existence of 'goodness' or 'badness' in [themselves] as well as in [their] mother."[10] They play out this theme in different ways. It may involve "good baby–bad baby" games, "good guy–bad guy" roles, or, as in the following anecdote, a girl's being "bad" herself.

Jessica rushed over to Jamie, quickly grabbed the car from his hand, darted across the room, and hid behind the teacher. When she saw Jamie rushing toward her, yelling "Jamie's car!", Jessica dropped the car and ambled over to a toy telephone. Picking up the receiver, she shouted, "Bad girl! You are a bad girl! Bad girl! You are such a bad girl!"

This play helped Jessica, who was having difficulty leaving her mother, come to terms with the good as well as the bad in herself. A short time after this incident, the teacher told her mother that Jessica had become a full-fledged class participant. Though the "bad" behavior resurfaced, it was short lived. Her entry into school was both positive and enthusiastic.

Jessica swooped into the classroom, ran over to Jamie, and snatched a small car from his hand. When Jamie protested loudly "No!" and half-rose to his feet, Jessica dropped the car, ran over to her cubby, skillfully unzipped her coat, and hung it on the hook. She rushed over to the shelf, picked up a toy car, plopped down next to Jamie, and pushed her car next to his. They played successfully with the cars together for a long time.

The younger the children the less able they are to use fully developed play in their attempts to gain mastery over their feelings. Children two and under are more directly imitative than symbolic in their play, yet this form of play gives them a chance to express themselves. Rebecca, nineteen months old, had spent most of the day in the center in a happy frame of mind.

After lunch, several children arrived at the center with their parents for the afternoon session. As one after the other of the parents bid goodbye to their children, Rebecca began to cry. She stood near the door, sobbing, repeatedly waving "bye-bye" and throwing kisses.

In reenacting the morning parting from her own parents, Rebecca gave vent to feelings that she had been containing. Her expression of such deep emotion drew the caregiver to her, and she accepted the comfort of a lap and a hug.

Play can also take the form of interacting with materials such as blocks, paints, crayons, water, or play dough. Through the creation of something with these materials, children are able to externalize some of their worry about separation. For example, three-year-olds often fear masks. They frequently believe that a mask is real and that the person wearing it is, indeed, a wolf, monster, or witch. They are equally afraid of putting on a mask. Perhaps they believe that if they do, they will change identity or disappear. They may believe, when they see a teacher or their parent put on a mask, that she has disappeared and has now become the witch or wolf. Here there are similarities with separation. The younger a girl or boy, the less able he or she is to understand that when a person leaves, he or she does not disappear. So it is with masks. While most four-year-olds understand that a person still exists beneath the mask, many three- and two-year-olds are just as sure that he or she does not. Thus, for a three-year-old, making a mask and being in charge of putting it on and taking it off in front of a mirror may be one way of adding some understanding about the appearance-disappearance aspects of separation.

Isaac came close to the paper bag masks that his brother and sister were making. He seemed frightened and started to back away. He watched intently as his father put on a mask. When he looked through the holes in the bag and saw his father's face, he laughed. He placed a paper bag over his own head and looked at himself in the mirror. He began to decorate the bag with his brother's felt-tip markers. He became relaxed and thoughtful. Finished, he sang out, "I made a mask!" patting his chest for emphasis. He gazed at his father and shouted with glee, "I made this. I'm gonna scare you!"

Children use the theme of appearance-disappearance in a variety of ways. Peek-a-boo is an age-old favorite that children begin to play as early as six or seven months of age. In those early months, the game allows the baby to experiment with the permanence of things and people. First you are here, then you are gone, and now you are back again! It is a way of learning that things and people exist even though they are not in sight. Babies play it again and again; learning that there is stability in the world takes a long time.

This game also allows young children to develop the means for coping with separation. In essence, separation is, after all, "You're here, you're gone, and now you're back." Peek-a-boo is both a rehearsal for and a recapitulation of the separation experience.

There are many variations on the theme of peek-a-boo. A two-year-old who wraps and unwraps his play dough with a large sheet of paper is playing the game in his own style. The following anecdote reveals how Jamal, a two-year-old who had a hard time separating from her mother, plays out some of her feelings with a small covered box containing a toy bear and a tiny blanket.

Jamal cried hard for a long time after her mother left. When she finally calmed down, her eyes lit on a small box. She opened it and grinned when she saw the bear inside. Removing the bear and the tiny blanket, she laid them both on the floor. Then she put the bear back in the box. "He's crying," she said, as she patted him. The box fell over and the bear rolled out. "Do you want to go to sleep in there?" Putting the bear back in, she said, "I cover him up." She closed the box and carried it as she walked around. Again she put it on the floor, opened it, and took the bear out. Rubbing her fingers over the bear, she put him back in and closed the cover. Opening the cover, she patted the bear three times and said, "G'night."

In comforting the crying bear, Jamal seemed to be reenacting both the feelings she had when she cried as well as the comforting she received from her caregiver. In the ritual of opening and closing the box, taking the bear in and out, she may have been reassuring herself that her mother, though gone, would come back. A significant aspect of this play situation is that the child has the upper hand. It is the child who says goodbye, who does the leaving, who controls the appearance and disappearance. This sort of spontaneous play adds to a child's growing sense of self-reliance.

When Parents Return

We have been focusing our attention on children when they are left by their parents. However, we must not neglect the reunion of parents and children at the end of the class session, at the end of the day, after a vacation or any brief separation. What happens then is often revealing and frequently misunderstood.

Have you ever had an experience like this? You come to call for your son at his center, expecting a warm and loving greeting at the end of the school day. No such thing happens! The boy refuses to leave, runs around the room, begins to paint or take blocks off the shelf, tries to put on dress-up clothes, or insists that the teachers now need his help in cleaning up the room. You lose patience and insist that he come home immediately. He goes reluctantly.

Or perhaps your child starts to cry when you return, or refuses to speak to you, or turns away from your attempts at a hug or a kiss.

What could be operating here? You might begin to think that your child likes school better than home or likes the teacher or caregiver more than you. That is seldom the case.

All during the day, children have been actively managing their angry or sad feelings about being left. When the end of the day comes, they find it hard to maintain that coping stance, and they may break down. Crying shows that they have reached their limit of dealing with these feelings and that now you are here, it is safe to express them. It is a declaration of love. Refusal to go home, giving you a hard time, and acting as if they do not wish to greet you in a loving way are all behaviors that say, in effect, "You left me here this morning. Now it's *my* chance to leave *you* by staying here. Now I can be in control of this situation. I can call some of the shots myself."

While in most cases a child's occasional avoidance of parents at reunion time is normal, there are extreme cases that might warrant further examination. If a child consistently, over a long period of time, ignores or rejects his or her parents, on leaving as well as on arriving, this may be a cause for concern. A small percentage of the children in the studies done by Dr. Mary Ainsworth[11] refused to respond to their mothers at reunion, ignored them, or rejected their attempts at greeting. Because of the persistence of this phenomenon, she labeled such children as ambivalent in their feelings toward their mothers or as "insecurely attached." If you have such a concern, it is best to discuss it with the teacher or seek help from a child guidance center or a child psychologist. Attending to problems of this nature when children are young is often more helpful than waiting until children are older and the problem has become more entrenched.

Other Separation Reactions

Separation reactions do not always go away after children have happily settled in a classroom. They may appear in a variety of other situations. You may be surprised to see some of the old behaviors appearing in a related context. For example, your daughter may be a four-year-old. As she begins to near her fifth birthday, you may notice an increased anxiety in talk about kindergarten, either with you or with her friends. A worry may creep in. Many four-year-olds believe that on the very day they become five they will go to kindergarten. They begin to suffer the separation blues until they understand that they will not have to leave the security of their present school or center immediately but can finish out the year with the rest of their classmates.

As entry to kindergarten becomes a reality, parents can prepare their children for the transition from nursery school or day care. They can talk about what the new school experience will be like—describing the toys, mentioning that there is a bathroom and a place to put coats. Encourage children to express their concerns so that you can clear up any misconceptions. Adults must serve as role models for children, Patricia Ziegler advises. "Adults help," she writes, "when they express similar feelings of their own and show appropriate ways to react to these new or confusing emotions."[12] She suggests that parents also focus on children's growth, such as the clothing or shoes they have outgrown and the skills they have acquired that they didn't have when they were younger. Since children grow very close to their preschool teachers over the years, Ziegler recommends asking the teacher for specific convenient times when a child might phone her over the summer or after kindergarten starts. A visit to the kindergarten is recommended.

Feelings about separation may erupt in situations that remind children of their original school separation experience. A resurgence of clinginess or a renewal of crying may occur when children return to school after an illness or a school vacation, or when a parent has gone away on—or even just returned from—a trip. It is as though they were going through a shortened version of their first school entry. There may also be a revival of these reactions when the teacher returns to the classroom after having been away for a time. It is not unusual for children to express angry feelings toward their teacher for having been away, no matter the reason for the absence.

Elizabeth refused to call her kindergarten teacher by name after the teacher returned from a week's absence. Miss Lawson had gone on a honeymoon and now was to be called Mrs. Gregory. Despite all the teacher's preparatory discussion with the children about the wedding and her change of name, Elizabeth was still angry at her and told her mother, "I don't like Miss Lawson anymore."

Mondays and Fridays can also be stressful times for parents and young children in group or home care. Leaving home after the weekend to go to the center, or saying goodbye to mom or dad at home when the sitter comes on Monday can be hard. Oddly enough, Fridays become tense as well because children then have to part from the center or the sitter. Added to this are parents' own feelings about Mondays and Fridays. It is clear why these days can be especially emotional.

Your reaction to your child will be important. Accepting these feelings with understanding aids a child's knowledge that certain emotions are appropriate. Accepting these feelings with understanding builds empathy between you—and empathy lies at the heart of close, productive family relations.[13] A mother describes such closeness:

When I leave for work in the morning my three-year-old often says, "I want to give you something to take to work with you." She disappears into her room and comes back with a doll, toy, or book for me. Sometimes I might request to trade it in for something smaller, but I always show her how I carefully pack it in my work bag. She seems content then that she has provided well for me for the day.

Some parents find that establishing a certain ritual around saying goodbye is very useful and predictable for youngsters. Here is one mother's routine with her son:

Max runs down the hall in front of me as we approach the front door of our apartment. He opens the door and we play a peek-a-boo game, opening and shutting the door. Then we both go to the elevator and say "See you later, alligator!" as it arrives and I step inside. The caregiver waits for him by the apartment door.

Similar separation reactions are frequently seen at the end of the school term. Children are not very ceremonious about saying goodbye to their teachers at that time, even though parents often urge their children to take a proper parting. Teachers and parents both sometimes feel let down when children blithely skip out the door on the last day without so much as a backward glance. One teacher I know found herself in tears as the last child nonchalantly left the room. Often young children simply cannot comprehend that they will not be coming back the following week. A parent may be surprised when her child asks "Why aren't I going to school today?" and school has been over for some time. Adults and preschool children have completely different understandings of and experience with time.

Some children do feel the pain of parting on the final day but do not know how to express it. The following record of a child's last day is a good example of the mixed feelings of anger and sadness that many of us, children and adults, feel when an important event draws to a close.

At the final day family picnic, Janine passes by her two teachers who are seated on a blanket. She shoots a quick glance at them and runs to her father. She returns in a few moments with a ball and starts to play—still not too close. Although the teachers speak to her, she does not look at them. When they ask her to sit with them, she gives them a hostile stare. Abruptly, she runs across the grass to a table where slices of watermelon are available. Gazing wistfully at her teachers from that distance, she eats her watermelon. Slowly she approaches, again appearing nonchalant, pointedly not responding to their remarks. She refuses to join them on their blanket, but sits on the grass, her back to them. Suddenly, she turns and says, over her shoulder, "Hey, I'm scrapin' this watermelon like an artichoke!" Showing her teachers the rind, she scrapes it with her teeth. Then just as suddenly, her face becomes downcast and she crawls up between the two teachers, and touching both, curls up and puts her thumb in her mouth.

How You Can Help

Your own keen observations of your child's behavior are a most fruitful source of knowledge. Sometimes parents' expectations of how their children *should* behave interfere with their "seeing" what is actually happening. We as adults have so much at stake in the way our children behave in public, especially in school. We would always prefer situations such as school entrance to go smoothly—not to be embarrassed by a clinging, crying, or protesting child. Remember that teachers see this sort of behavior year after year—it's not news to them, though it may be to you.

As you observe and accept your child's style in separating from you, you will be in the best position to be helpful. Coping with stress and gaining mastery over feelings are important requisites for maturing. Insisting that children must "tough it out" or "grow out of it" does not provide them with the opportunity to work through their feelings. In an environment of understanding and support, children become com-

It is you, the parent, who can do most for your child when she enters a classroom for the first time. Your support and caring helps her to grow toward independence.

petent and self-confident. They learn not only how to leave, but how to venture out—how to try new things.

When you say, "I know how you feel when I leave. We will both miss each other, but I will be back and I know your teacher will take good care of you," you are helping your children understand that their feelings of loneliness and grief are both legitimate and acceptable. You are helping them cope with those feelings through your love. You are helping them understand that their feelings have an end as well as a beginning. You are helping them master feelings by putting those feelings into words. You are helping them know that you have confidence in them. Your support helps them cope with those feelings and receive help from others. You and their teacher start them on their way to becoming sturdy and happy, able to function successfully in a safe, nurturing, and trustful environment. It is you, the parent, who has provided your child with this possibility for growth and with the potential for coping successfully with many future separations.[14]

Chapter 4

THE TEACHER'S ROLE IN BUILDING SELF-RELIANCE AND STRENGTH

Children need to learn that adults can be teaching, loving, and helping people. Teachers show children this through daily actions, courtesies, and gestures that do not detract from children's feelings of competence. Such actions by adults will help children want to grow up like the caring adults around them.[1]

What is the school's role? What can teachers do to encourage children's attempts at coping so that they emerge from their school separation experiences as strong, capable, and self-reliant individuals? How can teachers use their curriculum to fortify these children?

What is the meaning of "curriculum" for very young children? It is not something that is determined apart from the classroom. Rather it is based on the developmental abilities and needs of each child in the class. Curriculum for young children is what happens between the teacher and children, among the children themselves, and between the children and the activities, events, and materials provided by the teacher.

76

Curriculum is not merely a series of lesson plans or "recipes" for what to do in each situation that arises in classroom life. Preschool curriculum is not a predetermined list of activities in which children must participate.

Water play, for example, a staple in early childhood classrooms, cannot be described as effective curriculum apart from the teacher. As curriculum it depends on how teachers set it up, how they understand its value, how they mediate between the children and the uses children make of water, and what their reasons are for offering it to the children. If the teacher stands near the water play area, mopping up every spill, admonishing children to be careful, or directing children in how to use the water, he or she is providing one kind of curriculum. If the teacher allows the children to explore the water freely in their own ways, perhaps covering the table with toweling to minimize spills and encouraging the children to clean up by themselves, then he or she is providing a very different kind of curriculum, and a different experience for the children.

Separation can be considered as a curriculum process rather than as a single event. Imagine curriculum as a necklace with several strands of beads. One of those strands is called "separation." It stretches from the beginning of the school year to the end and is dotted with beads representing different activities. However, no one bead alone makes up the strand, as no one strand makes up the necklace. As teachers begin to provide children with activities to alleviate their separation stress, they also provide for them emotionally by means of their knowledge of the psychological roots of attachment and separation and their ongoing concern for children's positive growth and development. The teacher and the children are the strand upon which the beads are strung.

Let us, at this point, reexamine the characteristics of separating children described in Chapter 3 in order to reflect on curriculum decisions that teachers might make.

Children Who Are "Too Good"

Children like this are often hard for teachers to reach because working toward a relationship with them demands so much time and energy. This is admittedly troublesome because teachers have numbers of children clamoring for their attention. These quiet "good" children do not always make speedy progress, and it may take many weeks of reassurance and the teacher's continuing attention until they are able to function on their own. Parent-teacher cooperation, as described in Chapter 5, may be needed.

These children often require interchanges with the teacher alone before they are able to relate to other children. Stories read while the child sits on the teacher's lap, games played with the teacher, and clean-up chores done together are opportunities for intimate contact that builds a trusting relationship.

The following excerpts from a teacher's two-month observational log give an inside view of her work with one of these "good" children.

11/10 Diana seems to love the affectionate attention of other children, but she is not yet ready to interact with them. She does not seem to have a strong voice of her own yet. Her sparse language, her tentative steps may indicate that Diana does not feel entirely comfortable about classroom life.

Young children often need a trusting relationship with an adult before they can explore relationships with other children or take part in activities.

11/13   Diana still seems not quite in school. She has a faraway expression and roams around, touching a puzzle, a book, but can't seem to settle anywhere. "Would you like to do something with me?" I ask. She looks pleased and shakes her head "yes." We choose a stacking toy. She climbs on my lap, nuzzles into my arms, leans against me, puts her hand on my knees and I hear her breathe deeply.

11/20   Diana is using puppets, singing a song that comes from deep inside her, "La la la la." They are a very useful prop to get Diana out of her withdrawn state. She is really able to show a wide range of feelings, and the puppets have helped her get on with her language development. It may also seem as if the verbal interaction and the affectionate demonstration with momma and baby puppet helped Diana to deal with her separation feelings. She brought momma into the classroom when she needed her. A giant step for Diana.

11/26 Diana was very engrossed using crayons and paper. "Look," she said, "I made a girl." It was indeed a representation. The first she had done in school.

Later she began to tie her shoe. After much effort and concentration, she got the two loops together. Excitedly she flew over to me. "I tied my shoes myself!"

The two incidents, so close to each other, are further proof of Diana's growth.

12/11 I thought it would help finalize their separation if Diana could see her mom get on the school elevator each morning and watch the door close. This kind of sequencing seems to help Diana. It gave her a certain amount of control over the separation, rather than being *merely* left.

12/15 Today is Monday—sometimes hard to say goodbye. When Diana came back from walking her mom to the elevator, she wore that old faraway look. "You have that look that says you weren't ready to say goodbye to mommy." She smiled a half smile. "Sometimes mommies have to say goodbye too soon and you have to say goodbye too fast." Diana grasped my hand. It must have felt good to be understood.

Later in the day, Diana was constructing a body of clay. "I made a girl . . . arms, legs, eyes, nose, and a tushie." She said it with awe. I had the feeling that now Diana had a greater sense of herself as a separate person. She has all these separate parts. This was an important observation of her.

12/18   Both my assistant and I feel that she is more ready to be in school now. She has begun to move away from adults and play with children.

12/19   Diana is really blooming these days. She seems to experience herself as a separate person. I feel that since I started this log she has been gaining strength. The log has helped me focus on Diana and give her more of the support she needs.

Through this log we see Diana emerging from her silence and her "good" exterior, becoming a person related to others and more comfortable with herself. Her growth occurred because her teacher fully believed that separation was a significant part of the curriculum for this child. The teacher's use of her own interactions with Diana, her empathy with how Diana was feeling, her one-to-one reading of books, her use of puppets, and her attention to the ritual of Diana's goodbye to her mother were all concrete actions that formed curriculum. This log illustrates that curriculum for young children is what is planned, what is thought, and what happens.

If you think that your child might be "too good" in school, do you suspect that perhaps a part of him or her might never have come to school—that part might have stayed with you at home or at work?

If this example of Diana reminds you of your own child, you might take some cues from this teacher and try some of her techniques at home.

Delayed Reaction: Children Who Are "Fine," Then Fall Apart

How does the preschool curriculum serve children who seem "fine" the first few days or weeks and then fall apart? Some of the same things that strengthened Diana were appropriate—being read to, attended to during times of transition from one activity to the next, held on teachers' laps, sat next to at eating times, talked with often, sung with, played with frequently, and observed carefully.

You may think that so much attention to one child might jeopardize the teacher's relationship with the other children. On the contrary, the others will feel reassured when they see the teacher ministering to one child's needs. It is when a distressed child is *not* appropriately attended that other children become anxious and worried. They may have jealous feelings, but they will also feel that the teacher can take care of them, too, if they are feeling unhappy.

Sometimes a teacher may try all of these things and find that none of them works. A child is still upset, crying, without joy or pleasure in the classroom. This may be the point at which the teacher feels the need for an exploratory talk with the parent. The teacher may believe that the parent's presence in the classroom again is needed, and if the parent is free to come back she or he may be of two minds. On the one hand, the parent may be willing to help in any way that seems reasonable, as Kelly's mother was able to do. On the other hand, he or she may believe that the child must "get over it," and that the parent's return to the classroom will only make things worse.

If a parent is able to stay in the classroom again

and the situation does, indeed, get worse, it may be that the child is not really ready for school or group experience at all. In such a case a parent might consider delaying the start of school for a few months, if possible. Sometimes a breathing space gives both parent and child time to work through together some of the tensions surrounding the separation.

What is truly difficult here is the natural tendency to feel that you and your child have "failed." We adults often have definite ideas that equate "growing up" with "school." It is very hard to accept our child's inability to go to school in any terms other than failure. However, there is no such thing as failure in school entry. There may be only a slipping back, which requires help and often, more time.

If you are working outside your home and cannot return to the classroom, more creative measures may be required to help your child. The teacher may need to take an even more active role in providing surrogate parenting while the child is in school. Other actions may help:

- Arrange to phone your child at different times during the day
- Keep a favorite object from home available at the center for your child
- Make sure your child has access at school to a photograph of the family (put it in the cubby or lunchbox)
- Make an audio tape of yourself reading a favorite story for the child to play in school
- Invite the teacher for a visit to your home
- Request extra conferences with the teacher
- Tell the teacher what the child's favorite activities are so she can do them in school

Perhaps a talk with your employer about the need for

a bit of extra time off to help your child in school will yield a positive result.

Children Who Regress in Their Behavior

At school beginning it is common to see children thumb sucking, having toilet accidents, talking very little or too much, not eating at all or overeating, becoming clumsy, clinging to special objects, refusing to nap, becoming aggressive, showing a lack of self-confidence, or being unable to play.

What are some special techniques that are useful for giving children comfort during the first few weeks of school? How can parents and teachers support children's regressive behavior and help them, at the same time, move toward self-confidence? Many of the suggestions made in connection with children who are too good and those who display a delayed reaction also apply to those whose behavior has regressed. No matter what kinds of signals a child sends out, encouraging their expressions of feeling is the most significant contribution you can make to their growth. In the words of one expert, "The child who really copes well allows himself to miss the absent loved one, to feel sad, lonely and perhaps angry, and to express his feelings appropriately."[2]

Children With Particular Needs

Children have a variety of needs stemming from particular circumstances. For example, some children come from single-parent homes, from homes with recently separated parents, from homes where there has been a death or chronic or serious illness of a loved person or pet. Some children's parents might be depressed. Some parents are adolescents. Some children have disabilities, either psychological or physical. Any such circumstances may influence the character of the parent-child separation. While it is true that these kinds of differences should be minimized rather than exaggerated, children may require special attention as they separate. If any of these situations relates to your particular circumstance, you may want to discuss it with the teacher before your child enters her classroom. In this way, you and the teacher may be able to pave a smooth way for a good beginning.

In a program for mildly retarded children, for example, it was noted that the children did not give the same kinds of clues to their feelings about separation as nonretarded children.[3] Their regressive behavior was often attributed to the retardation itself, and the children's aimless running around to hyperactivity. As the mothers began to recognize their children's feelings of anxiety about separation, they also began to understand the depth of their children's attachment to them. The teachers made special efforts to help the children identify themselves by "showing [them their] own photograph, saying [their] name and verbally calling attention to what [they were] doing."[4] Then they attempted to develop in the child the same awareness of "mother." They talked about "where she is now, what she is doing, and the reunion with her."[5] The teachers continually encouraged the expected, normal response to separation on the part of the children, and in so doing enlisted the mothers' cooperation. Concreting the separation process and the child's identity helped these children, since they lacked conceptualizing skills.

Activities That Help Children Cope with Separation

There are many ways that parents and teachers can help children express their feelings about separation and cope with their emotions. One way is to meet the feelings head-on and talk about them.

Frank Langella, the actor, helped his four-year-old son conquer the monster who invaded the boy's room at night.[6] For several weeks after the initial appearance of the monster, Langella "did a dutiful daddy fight with the monster . . . driving him back out into the night," but "[no] matter how hard I battled, the monster returned when my son wanted him to." When Langella thought back to a mummy who had come to get him when he was a child and the mummy's "eventual disappearance," he "realized that [the mummy] had never really gone away. He was with me still. He changed shapes as rapidly as I grew up. He became a wild bear at the foot of my bed . . . In later years, he was my first day at kindergarten . . . He was hypodermic needles . . . Still later, my first date, my first night away from home, at sixteen, alone in a small boardinghouse as an apprentice in summer stock."

When his son screamed again in the night he went in, turned on the light and told him that "I was never going to kill the monster again. I explained that this was his monster. He had made him up and only he could kill him. I said that he could make him go away whenever he chose, or that he could turn him into a friendly monster if he liked . . . I said that I would no longer perform this particular battle for him, but that I loved him and would always love him. A slow and overwhelmingly beautiful smile that I shall never forget came to his face and he said: 'You mean, I can make him do anything I want?' 'Yes,' I said, 'you're in charge of him.' ''

"As my son grows," he concluded, "I know we will be able to face his monsters together. And now, when all I was once so sure of has become a mystery to me, I'm hoping he'll be able to help me face the unknown ones yet to visit themselves upon me.''

In helping their children confront feelings like these and gain control of them, parents supply powerful tools for living.

Ways That Parents Can Prepare Their Children

Knowing that your son or daughter will soon be starting school or day care, what can you do at home to prepare for the event?

Tell your child in advance—but not too far ahead—that he or she will soon be going to school or day care. Paint a positive picture of the forthcoming experience but be careful not to go overboard with enthusiasm.

Reassure your child that the school you have chosen is a good place for children and that it has your stamp of approval. Never send your child to a school or center that does not insist that you visit first.

Do not use school as a means to make children change their behavior or become toilet trained. Children must believe that they are right for school *just the way they are*.

Examine your own feelings. What is the balance between worry and excited anticipation? If excitement predominates, share some of that with your child in casual talk about the center. If worry predominates, try to examine your concerns, or discuss them with the teacher or the director before school starts, if possible. This sort of worry often filters its way down to the child.

If the school has a "paint and get ready" spruce-up session before the fall opening, volunteer your services if you can. It will give you a chance to feel comfortable in the setting and to get to know a few people. There may also be opportunities for children to help by putting clean toys on the shelves, washing tables and chairs, helping to mount pictures, or putting labels on cubbies. Such activities add a measure of child-control over the physical environment and afford children some familiarity with the room. Teachers, children, and parents can begin to know one another.

Other Ways You Can Help

During beginning days of the program, your child can choose a spot in the room for you to sit while you are watching.

If you need to stay in the classroom for any length of time, you might suggest to your child, when she goes into the schoolyard with the teacher and the group, that you will wait in the room. In that way, the child leaves the parent, rather than the reverse.

Allow your son or daughter to move toward the teacher or caregiver at his or her own pace. Children need to feel their way in new situations. Dr. J. Ronald Lally found in a 1985 study three influences on children's reactions to parting:

(1) If the new caregiver waited at a distance from the child without moving in too quickly, the child responded better than if the adult rushed in and picked up the child.

(2) The caregiver's use of a toy to make indirect contact with the child was better than touching or making direct eye contact, which resulted in the child's clinging to the parent.

(3) If the caregiver and mother were alike in appearance and mothering style, the child adjusted more quickly to the caregiver. This did not mean that the child couldn't "warm up to someone very different from mother—it simply took more time."[7]

Encourage your child to participate fully in saying goodbye, whether you are parting at home or at school. Hugging, kissing, crying, waving, and saying "I'll miss you, I love you" are all ways of bringing feelings about separation out into the open. Once in the open, they are easier to deal with. Never sneak out— while it may be more comfortable for you to avoid a "scene," it may make children feel abandoned and unloved.

In a study of children's reactions to separation,[8] children whose mothers slipped out, giving them no information about their leaving or projected return, showed the most distress. Those whose mothers provided them with information about where they were going and when they would return, and in addition, suggested activities for the children during the mother's absence, showed less distress.

Do not place your preschool child or toddler on a bus for the first day at school, unless you ride, too. It is very frightening for young children, who do not understand that someone will greet them at the end of the ride. It is also impossible for teachers and parents to develop a relationship if they never, or seldom, meet.

Talk with your child about her feelings, even if you do not think she understands or is listening. This will enable her to eventually take verbal steps toward mastery of her emotions and control of her actions,[9] as Frank Langella's son was able to do.

Plan with your child, if necessary, for the next day's parting. Through their inclusion in such planning, children gain security and experience self-confidence.

Request that the teacher or caregiver provide an opportunity for your son or daughter to watch you leave. Perhaps there is a window through which a child can peer to wave goodbye. Steps placed by a high window allow children to look into the street as parents leave the building.

Regard all the "baby ways" that may appear, from thumb sucking to wet pants, without a fuss. The less attention you pay to such behaviors, even if they bother you, the sooner they will disappear.

Support your child's desire to bring a favorite toy or blanket, or something belonging to you, to school each day. Explain to the teacher that this particular "security" object is very special and that your son or daughter need not share it with other children. To children, such objects are a bit of home.

Letters Help your child write a letter that you keep with you. This is meaningful to three-, four- and five-year-olds. Setting down "I will see you after my nap, I miss you, I love you" in words on paper seems to be very reassuring. The letter can contain a drawing or the child's own "writing." Your child might like such a letter from you that could be kept in his cubby or in his pocket.

Photographs Photographs of the family, including pets, grandparents, aunts, uncles, cousins, and important neighbors, posted in an accessible spot like a school cubby, or tucked into a lunchbox, help young children remember that their families really do exist,

A stuffed animal helps when a child is feeling lonely.

Photographs of the family remind a toddler that though out of sight, mom and dad still exist.

even though they cannot be seen. Covering these photographs with adhering plastic will assure their withstanding lots of loving attention.

A Storybook Write a story with your child about going to school. Include photographs if possible. Begin with the child's getting up in the morning and getting ready for school. Continue with the trip to school and saying goodbye. Describe the activities that the child enjoys during the day and end with your arrival at school in the afternoon and your pleasure at seeing one another again. Mat board, purchased in an art supply store, makes a very sturdy book for a young child. It can be held together with binder rings.

Another storybook, about what you are doing while your son or daughter is in school or day care, might be meaningful. Such a book could show, through photographs and texts, what some of your activities are at work or at home. Books of this sort form a valuable link with home that a young child can carry about and look at whenever necessary.

Playing Using puppets helps four- and five-year-old children express their feelings about separation and missing you. Children this age are attracted by animal puppets and often label them mommy, daddy, grandma, baby, and so on. They will need your help. Your puppet will have to ask their puppet some questions to get the play going. "Hello!" yours might say. "Are you going to school today? I'll bet you have fun there. What sorts of things do you do? Where is your mommy (daddy, grandma) while you are in school?" You may find yourself included in the play and perhaps assigned a role.

Games of peek-a-boo and games of hiding and retrieval can be played in sand and water where toys can be hidden and found easily. This is fun for children when they take a bath. It is a way of practicing being left and being reunited. Such games give children control over the process of leaving and returning. Perhaps that is why a jack-in-the-box is so popular with youngsters.

Provide for, and observe, children's natural dramatic play. This may give you consistent clues as to how children are doing in their attempts to cope with separation reactions. Both boys and girls may play baby or nurturing parent many times over in their attempts to come to terms with their feelings. They may play themes of moving or going on trips. They may play monster as they begin to face their fears of being on their own in school. Parents can provide for children's make-believe by supplying props such as discarded suitcases, some dolls, a doll bed large enough

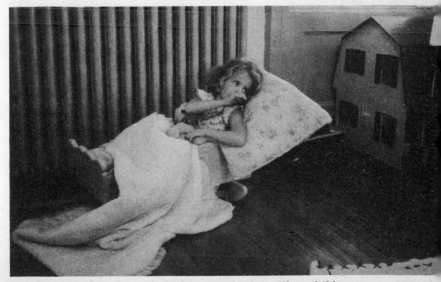

Playing baby in the doll bed is comforting. This child uses make-believe in her efforts to master her feelings.

Taking on a role enables children to experiment with another identity while strengthening their own.

for a child to lie on (often a sturdy cardboard box will do just as well), lengths of cloth, pillows, hats, old pocketbooks, shoes, and space for play. If you discreetly listen to, but don't intrude on, such play, you may discover just what means children use to cope with their feelings. You may get to know your child even better.

Expressive materials If you can, try to provide some "nonstructured" materials, such as paints, blocks, clay, play dough, crayons, felt-tip markers, and clean paper for drawing. These activities are best set up in the kitchen where spills or unwanted marks can be most easily wiped up. Use of these materials (free of all adult direction about what to make) allows children to spontaneously represent their feelings about themselves, their families, and their entry into the new world of school. Some of those feelings may not be pleasant, and it will help if you are prepared to see—and accept—both angry and sad feelings being displayed.

Books Storybooks about how it feels to be separated from a loved one can open the way for children and

Children make an impact on a blank piece of paper. It is a way of saying "I am me—a separate, special person."

Satisfaction, a feeling of accomplishment, and a sense of competence come from the joyful involvement with nonstructured play materials.

parents to talk together about separation, gaining new insights into the process.

Choosing these books should be done with care. The first consideration is that the book be good literature. It should be pleasurable for you to read and pleasurable for your child to hear. Does the book display clarity of writing style, brevity, interesting characters, and suitable illustrations? Be certain that the book is free of stereotypes. It must also appeal to you—it is very unsatisfying to read to a child if the book is uninteresting to the reader.

Books that address sensitive topics like separation need other special qualities. In an article about the use of books in crisis situations, adults are are urged to apply the following guidelines:

Can children identify with the plot, setting, dialogue, and characters?

Does the book use correct terminology, psychologically sound explanations, and portray events accurately? . . .

Are the origins of emotional reactions revealed and inspected? . . .

Does the book reflect an appreciation for individual differences? . . .

Does the book present crises in an optimistic, surmountable fashion? . . .[10]

How you read the book to your child is critical. First, be thoroughly familiar with the book before you read it to your son or daughter. If you are feeling tense or anxious about the separation process, wait until you are more relaxed to read the story. Otherwise it will be hard for the child to relate the book to her feelings—she will be caught up in yours. You might mention some naturally occurring incident that may have prompted the book's use. Comments, or questions, casually made throughout or after the story "encourage children to analyze the behavior of the story characters, make inferences about emotional reaction, apply information to their own experience, and synthesize techniques for coping with crisis."[11] Finally, summarize the story by rephrasing the basic story concepts. In this way, children's ideas and information can be clarified.

An annotated booklist for children can be found on page 179–189.

Beginning Days

Beginning days and weeks are not the time for expecting trips or stimulating art projects in the center or school for young children. You may think that the program is getting off to too slow a start, but children need time to get acquainted with the teachers and with the room and its materials. Teachers need to plan carefully for these beginning days. There are many decisions that they need to make.

Teachers need to decide whether or not to put out all the blocks or just a limited number of shapes. The age of the children and their former experience with blocks will influence the teacher's decision. Very young children of three and under may be overwhelmed by more than just two or three basic shapes in the beginning. On the other hand, kindergarteners, who may be experienced builders, might feel cheated if the block shelves are not full.

Will the teacher start with several colors of paint or just one or two? Will she start with paint at all? Young toddlers may not be ready to use brushes and an easel in the early days of the program. They may need more time to control their small muscles, while older children may be ready right away to try their hands at painting.

Teachers need to make many decisions about equipping their classrooms in the beginning weeks. Many teachers tend to use less, rather than more. They will think about puzzles—shall there be hard as well as easy puzzles on the shelf? Will some children entering the group be highly skilled in puzzles? Will others get discouraged if the puzzles are out of their range?

Will the teacher provide paste with collage materials or wait until the children have been in the program for a while? The decision will most likely be based on the age and experience of the children as well as the amount of adult help available in the room. If teachers have to spend large amounts of time teaching children how to use paste in the early days, it may inhibit their more important interactions with parents and children.

Will the teacher put crayons or felt-tip markers, or both, on the table with the drawing paper? Markers are very easy to use and respond best to a light touch. The age of the children in the group and the kind of touch they use will influence the decision. An eighteen-month-old does not have the finesse of a five-year-old, so crayons are best at this age.

These teacher decisions convey specific messages to children and their parents. Be aware of them. A carefully arranged room with well-chosen materials in appropriate quantities reflects the teacher's serious attention to the needs of beginning days. When there is a certain order, a cheerful cleanliness, an array of attractive playthings that are not overwhelming, you will know that your arrival has been anticipated joyfully—and thoughtfully. The teacher's pleasure, and care, in the entry of children and their parents will help prepare the way for a successful separation.

Social Life

The social life of a classroom is a slowly evolving, ever-changing phenomenon. Today's enemies are tomorrow's friends. "You can't come to my birthday" frequently turns into "Do you want to play good guys and bad guys?" Teachers play an important role in helping young children learn what it means to be a friend when they demonstrate friendliness, compassion, and respect for children. This model of an adult who is an enabler[12] provides the most meaningful lesson to the young. In an atmosphere of acceptance, children learn to be accepting; in an atmosphere of empathy, children learn to be empathic; in an atmosphere that encourages autonomy, children learn to be autonomous.

The understanding of social life develops as chil-

Sometimes friendship takes unique forms.

dren's thinking abilities mature. In a study of friendship, children's ideas were shown to change as they became less egocentric*.[13] Whereas in early childhood a friend is regarded as valuable because "she has a Star Wars toy," children develop, by early teens, an understanding of the reciprocal nature of friendship.

Helping children as they struggle to comprehend what it means to get along with others is a demanding task for both parents and teachers. It is often more helpful for children to be asked, "What happened?" in a conflict situation than for the adult to decide who

*"Egocentric" is a term that describes young children's thinking. It is characterized by the assumption that the actions of people and events in the child's world are somehow magically connected to the child's self (ego). For example, a three-year-old eager to see snow asked "If I take a nap, will it snow?" as though her napping could influence natural events.

is at fault. Children need the opportunity to examine a situation and try to work out a solution with the parent's or the teacher's help. They need as much chance to play alone as with others because social life requires that people be in harmony with themselves as a foundation to harmony with others.

You can help young children define their separating selves by encouraging them to interact constructively with other children. By initiating and sustaining social interaction, parents and teachers build a bridge connecting children securely to the human world. As these experiences for children multiply, their trust in you and in their teachers flourishes because it is built on a firm foundation.

Encouraging Children's Competence

Parents and teachers can provide many opportunities for children to develop and exercise competence: teachers, through a curriculum that has an understructure of support for separating children; parents, through meeting children's needs for both attachment and autonomy. Helping children build self-confidence and self-reliance appropriately can make them feel comfortable and safe when they are away from the protection of their parents. The key word here is "appropriately." Even though two-year-olds, for example, might be able to do many things for themselves, it is not appropriate to assume that they never need holding or cuddling, or that they can solve interpersonal problems without the assistance of an adult.

The thrust for being capable, for making a difference in the world, for having an effect on the environment comes from within. It is said that such motivation is inborn.[14] You who are with your children day after

Competence is built in many ways:

through trying new foods,

through taking risks,

through developing new skills,

and through engaging with books.

day know firsthand about their intense drive to do things for themselves. "I do it myself!" is a phrase familiar to every parent of a young child. It begins when children are under two years of age, with their actions saying what their words cannot.

Encouraging this innate motivation builds competence in the young. There are many opportunities both at home and in the preschool classroom for this: in carrying out the routines of the day, such as pouring juice from a small, lightweight pitcher (a plastic eight-ounce measuring cup will do), dressing, choosing foods to eat, or toileting; in selecting toys (or art materials in school) to play with and getting them from the shelves oneself; in taking risks, making friends, and choosing books. Achievement fills a child with pride and self-gratification. It is fed by the comfort and trust generated in a secure classroom and home environment. Separation is the "developmental necessity" underlying the child's discovery of herself as a maker, a doer, a builder.

One of the most valuable contributions to your child's development will be your recognition that separation reactions are valid and expectable. Your own knowledge and your understanding of this as a significant element of early childhood will help your son or daughter develop a strong sense of himself as an individual able to feel sad, angry, and grieving. Your child will be able to develop the ability to cope with those feelings without being overwhelmed or rendered ineffective.

The steps children take to achieve this as they enter school will help them practice the skills they will use in many different separation experiences all through their lives.[15]

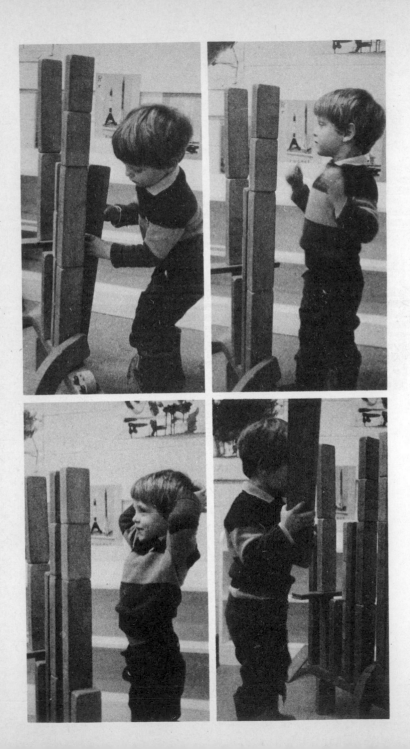

Achievement fills a child with pride and self-gratification. Separation is the "developmental necessity" underlying a child's discovery of himself as a builder.

Chapter 5

EASING THE BREAK: PARENTS AND TEACHERS WORKING TOGETHER

Parents, children, and teachers are equal participants in the drama of separation and school entry. Each group has needs that require attention. This chapter addresses the need of parents and teachers to learn from one another.

Every September newspapers carry stories about school openings that seem to verify the meaningful nature of this event. There are often photographs that dramatize the tension of starting school for children and parents. In the *New York Times* of September 14, 1982, Suzanne Daley wrote:

> The stuffed animal that goes everywhere with five-year-old Eric Benderisky went to Public School 9 yesterday. It was Eric's first day of school, and Puppy Dog's, too. Eric held one paw, and Eric's mother Ruth held the other, and that was the way they arrived at 100 West 84th Street. Eric said he was o.k. His mother said she was nervous.
>
> Elizabeth Sanchez kept her eyes on her son, Jason, 6, who had complained of a stomachache

before he left for school. "His older sister said some bad things to him about school, so he's scared," Mrs. Sanchez said.

Another school entry was described by Dena Kleiman in the *New York Times* of September 9, 1980:

Diana Lambouras, who had taken her five-year-old son, Emilio, to school for the first time yesterday, was standing in the rear of his classroom at P.S. 51. It as almost 2 p.m. and she had been standing there all day.

"I've tried to leave," Mrs. Lambouras explained. "But every time I do, he falls on the floor and starts screaming."

Mrs. Lambouras said she had asked her son this past weekend whether he wanted to go to school and when he had told her he did not, she said she had tried to change his mind.

"You'll learn to read and write, you'll make new friends," Mrs. Lambouras recalled saying. "You want to go to school, now don't you?'

" 'Yes,' " Mrs. Lambouras said her son had answered, " 'but you have to come with me.' "

Mrs. Lambouras agreed.

She said she planned to stay with Emilio today and even tomorrow . . . "But next week," she added, "he's on his own."

Perhaps some form of preparation might have made this first day more comfortable, more predictable. A visit to the school by the mother and her son in the spring, a meeting with the teacher prior to the school's opening, a written description of the school beginning mailed to the parent and child, a parents' meeting held before the actual opening took place might have contributed clarity and direction to the event. Perhaps a letter of welcome from the teacher to the boy would have been helpful. As a parent, you have the right to inquire whether or not any of these steps will be taken by the program your child will be attending.

With the youngest children, those under three, it is imperative that parents' and teachers' contact with one another be as ongoing, supportive, and close as it is with the children. When teachers think "children" of this age they should automatically think "parents." It is important that you expect this attitude in teachers of such very young children. Ask yourself whether the teacher respects the attachment that exists between yourself and your child. If the answer is yes, consider the program. If the answer is no, look elsewhere.

Every effort should be made by the school or center for you and the teacher to have contact before your son or daughter arrives in the classroom, or in the family day-care home. You need to see what sort of a person the teacher is and how he or she works with children. You need to know some of the teacher's ideas about child rearing and to decide whether or not you agree with them. You need to feel that the teacher is trustworthy and competent to take care of your dearest possession.

"It's a little bit difficult for parents," one parent wrote on a questionnaire, "because they are entrusting people they still don't know very well with what is most precious to them—their child."

In one center, parents are invited to observe the teacher in action with her present class before deciding whether to enroll their children. Such a preenrollment visit is actually the beginning of the separation process and is the first phase of the entry. The message to parents is (1) our center respects your judgment and your duty to know what kind of arrangements you are making for your child, and (2) we think our center is pretty wonderful and we want you to see it for yourself. Parents have every right to suspect that something is wrong with a center where no such visiting is allowed. This holds true for parents of three-, four-, and five-year-olds as well as the under-threes.

If you decide, after an initial visit, that you want your child in this center, you will have another opportunity to get to know the teacher. Some teachers may request a conference with you while others like to make a home visit if it is acceptable. Such a visit sometimes helps a young child feel more comfortable on arriving at school. "Oh, I saw you at my house!" is a familiar preschool greeting for the teacher. On the other hand, some parents find the idea of a home visit nerve-racking. Some feel that they will be judged on the basis of how their living quarters look. Others may consider it an invasion of their privacy. The choice of the home visit, if offered, must remain in the hands of the parent. You must be able to say no.

This first face-to-face contact is the second step in the entry and separation process. This conference and/or home visit might be held during the first two or three weeks of school. An initial conference might begin like this:

Ms. K. arrived for her first meeting with the teacher. Her three-year-old son Aaron would be starting school the following week. The teacher outlined the first week's schedule, explaining that he welcomed and expected Ms. K. to stay in the classroom with Aaron. He invited Ms. K. to the first parents' meeting, which was being held that evening. (Ms. K. had already received an invitation in the mail.)

"How are you feeling about Aaron's beginning school?" the teacher asked.

"Well, to tell you the truth," Ms. K. answered, "I'm excited. It's wonderful to see him becoming so independent and so grown up. But I'm a little nervous, too. You know, it's a new phase in our lives. I'm so used to leaving him at home with a babysitter when I'm at work. And I don't think my boss will let me take the day off to stay in the classroom."

"Other mothers have told me the same thing. So you can see that you're not alone in your feelings. Do you think your babysitter, or someone who knows your son well, could stay with him for a time in the beginning? Could you manage to come with both of them for a short time on the first day, just to put your stamp of approval on this center?"

"Well, I'm sure he'll be fine without me, but I suppose that the sitter, or my mother, could spend some time with him to help him get used to it here. I'll think about talking to my boss about coming in a little late on Aaron's first day."

The teacher and Ms. K. have just started to build their relationship. The teacher raised the issue of separation so that Ms. K. would have the opportunity to prepare herself and her son. He tried to make Ms. K. feel that her slight nervousness and her inability to stay were not unusual. He tried to make suggestions to accommodate her working situation. Ms. K. may have been trying to make the teacher feel that her son would be a "good boy." The groundwork has been set for the teacher and parent to begin to work together. Had it been possible for this parent to stay with her son, if she worked evenings or part-time, or had an approachable boss, or was a full-time homemaker, the teacher would have worked out with her a transition to the classroom suited to her schedule. The important aspect of these arrangements for beginnings is flexibility. A rigid method tends to create conflicts and misunderstanding.

Children Are Strangers

When children come to school for the first time, they are strangers. The teacher knows very little about them. They know very little about the teacher. The teacher has not had time yet to become sensitive to their cues—to become alert, for example, to that "look in Tina's eyes" foretelling that a storm may break.

During these beginning days teachers may have very little information to guide them, for children have many different ways of showing how they feel. Each child has his or her own behavior vocabulary. For example, two children may feel angry. One child may scream in rage; another may withdraw into a quiet, sullen shell. As teachers come to know the children over time, they begin to know which behavior, for which child, means what most of the time.

Although teachers depend on their intuitions and on their former experiences to understand the range of feelings they see children express, sometimes they are right in what they surmise, and sometimes they are wrong. Much of what they do in the beginning will be guesswork. For that reason, it is crucial at the time of a child's entry that teachers enlist the support of the parents, who truly know their child best.

Parents Are an Important Source of Information

This first meeting with the teacher, held before the program starts or at its beginning, is vital if the teacher is to learn about your child. It is also an opportunity for you to begin to know the teacher. Does he or she set a tone of friendliness? Is he a good listener? Is he open to your comments? Do you get the impression that the teacher sincerely wants your input about your child? Do you have the opportunity to share your concerns and wishes for your son or daughter with the teacher? Are you able to express your goals for your child in this program? A first conference should be a time for the teacher to gather information from you in order to know more about your child. It is up to the teacher to help you feel comfortable in this exchange.

Here are the type of questions that teachers may ask in this first conference with you:

What made you seek day care or nursery school for your child at this time?

What are your wishes and aspirations for your daughter?

What would you like me to know about your son's development?

What can you tell me about your child's pattern of eating and sleeping? About her usual routine at home?

How would you describe your daughter's personality and disposition? What do you like most about her?

Are there ways in which you would like her to change?

What would you like your son to get out of school?

The teacher's task in this interaction will also be to help you think about your decision to send your child to his or her classroom. She can do this by describing to you her program and the philosophy of the school or center so that you can decide whether or not you have made the right choice. Here are some questions that you might want to ask the teacher:

What do you consider the major goals of your program?

What is your point of view about children making choices? How do you put that into effect?

What is the range of materials available for the children's use?

Is there space and time for safe outdoor play?

What do you consider unacceptable behavior? How do you handle it?

What do you do if a child becomes ill or has an injury?

What is your approach to school entry and separation?

How Teachers Help Parents When School Begins

Parents should *expect* teachers to welcome them to stay with their children for the beginning day or days, or as long as they believe it necessary. While some parents may worry that they will not be allowed to stay at all, others may worry that they will be required to stay too long or that their children will never stay unless they, the parents, leave the school immediately.

There are ways that teachers can help parents strike a balance—neither too short nor too long a stay.

Does the teacher, or director, discuss the entry process and raise the issue of separation in your initial interview, either when you seek information about the school or before school starts? If not, raise the issue yourself. You need to know how the beginning will go for you and your child.

Is the teacher a good listener? Does he or she tune in to your concerns about your child's starting school? If you need to go to work, is the teacher receptive to working out a program for the beginning that accommodates you as well as your child? Does he or she provide you with the information that you are seeking? Do you feel comfortable asking questions? Does the educational philosophy fit with your ideas about child rearing?

Does the teacher convey to you that you will work together as partners for the benefit of your child? Does he or she ask you questions about your son or daughter that demonstrate an interest in taking cues from you as the person who knows the child best? It is important that you share information about how your child does in new situations so that the entry process can be as smooth and as successful as possible. If you anticipate any stress, bring it up so that you and the teacher can evolve a suitable plan.

Does the teacher have a plan for the first week or weeks, based on the age and needs of the children, and on your needs? The younger the children, the more time will probably be needed for them to feel safe. Is that plan made clear to you? Is it consistent throughout the school? Chapter 6, on school procedures, contains guidelines for your understanding the rationale for such plans.

Is there support for you and an arrangement to communicate with you each day in case it is truly impossible for you, or someone else close to your child, to stay with him or her? Are you able to work out a plan to help bridge the gap by making one or two phone calls from work to your child in the center?

It is entirely appropriate for you to count on supportive help from the teacher and the director of the school or center you have chosen for your child. The information you provide about yourself and your child will contribute to the teacher's effectiveness in working with you and your son or daughter.

Parents in the Classroom

Parents can support the teacher's efforts to learn about their children by being in the classroom the first few days of school. Parents have the opportunity then to give teachers intimate information about their children, such as the following:

George will stay by my side for a while watching what other children do, but then he'll make his way over to something that interests him.

Lauretta is such a social butterfly! You'll see that in no time at all she'll be talking up a storm with another child.

I'm afraid we're really going to have trouble with Harry. He never wants me to leave him. I don't know what I'm going to do.

Some parents may be more circumspect about what they say to the teacher. It is up to the teacher to try to help those who are more reticent about their children.

Parents Contribute to Children's Security

Research has shown that children are more exploratory and more openly social in an unfamiliar environment if they are accompanied by a familiar adult, usually a parent.[1] However, these children behaved quite differently in the same strange environment when their parents were not there. Rather than investigating the objects in the environment and exploring the space, some children showed distress by crying, thumb sucking, or stamping their feet. Others spoke less, stopped playing, or moved about hesitantly. With the familiar adult present, the children played, spoke, and moved about comfortably. Apparently the adults' presence was a secure base from which the children could wander and explore. These studies have been interpreted to mean that the adults' presence communicated a feeling of power to the children, while the adults' absence conveyed the children's powerlessness.

You can probably translate these research findings into your own life. Have you ever had the feeling, when embarking alone on a new adventure, that you would rather have had the company of a familiar person? Is it more comfortable for you to walk into a roomful of strangers with another, known person than by yourself? Do you remember going away to camp or college and feeling that you would have liked to have had one of your family members or a close friend with you, at least for a short time? Did you ever long for the comfort of your old home after you moved to a new location? These natural longings for familiarity in new and untried situations are a part of our human heritage.

Though young children feel safer with their parents nearby, they also have a great push from within to steer their own ship. "You're not the boss of me!"

The child's urge to be protected is strong.

I do it myself!

the four-year-old cries out against adult authority. "I do it myself!" the two-year-old shouts at offers of help. These conflicting tides are unsettling to children as well as to adults. While one urge pulls the child toward adult protection, the other propels the child away into a sea of her own actions. Even we as adults may experience conflicting feelings—wanting and simultaneously not wanting to be separate, independent, and autonomous; wanting and at the same time not wanting to be connected to or merged with another person.

Parents and Teachers Also Experience Conflict

Is it any surprise that when young children enter schools and centers, torn between wanting to leave their parents and wanting to hold on to them, that the adults, too, get caught up in the age-old dilemma? "The maturing adult," Louise Kaplan writes in *Oneness and Separateness,* "is continually reliving and revising his memories of childhood, redefining his identity, reforging the shape of his selfhood, discovering new facets of his being."[2] This conflict between wanting to be autonomous and wanting to be dependent exists to some degree in all adults. Surely you have felt that pull between the feeling that "I'd just like to go to bed, pull the covers over my head, and forget everything" and the feeling that "I can take care of it." These adult feelings have some similarity to the contrary pulls that children experience, especially when they enter school.

Recognition of this conflict is the important and necessary first step for parents and teachers. Young children and parents often need help from the teacher in resolving this conflict when children begin school. It is not always comfortable for teachers to do this.

While young children need their parents to help them make a comfortable transition from home to school, sometimes school rules serve just the opposite purpose. Consider the following:

Children are to ride the bus on the first day.
Seats are for children only.
Parents bringing children on the first day may stay for the first half hour only.

Such regulations send strong messages to parents that they are not wanted. It would benefit your child for you to question such rules.

All parents have feelings about their children's first days at school or group care that need to be recognized and supported by teachers. Parents also need to have control over their children's lives and to have a say in how their children will make the transition to school. Rules like these deny them this control, as do rules that dictate overly structured entry schedules. Arriving at an entry procedure that meets the needs of each parent and child is a challenging problem for schools and centers. How teachers and directors work with you in the first days will contribute to a spirit of either cooperation or competition. You can be on the alert and try to select a program in which cooperation is the dominant mode of relating.

Some Programs Use a Questionnaire

Some schools or centers ask parents to fill out a questionnaire before their child enters. One advantage of a questionnaire is the time for reflection that it offers—both to parents answering it and to teachers reading it. Some teachers ask parents to fill it out at home, while others may use the questionnaire as a guide for the first parent-teacher conference.

Still others may prefer to wait a few weeks, until they know you and your child a bit better, to ask that a questionnaire be answered.

Parents react differently to questionnaires. Some may enjoy filling them out while others may perceive them as an invasion of privacy. However, if the questionnaire is well designed, the answers will help teachers know children better and improve their work with them in the classroom. If there are questions that you believe are inappropriate, be sure to discuss your feelings about them with the teacher or the director. You have every right to ask the teacher about the ways in which he or she will use the information.

You will find a sample questionnaire for parents, with an explanation of the questions, at the end of this chapter.

A Parents' Meeting Before School Opens

A parents' meeting before school begins can ease the initial phase of school entry. In a day-care setting, where children enter at varied times during the year, such a meeting may be held within three months of your entry date.

A meeting focusing on school beginning and the separation of parent and child will validate this as an occasion meriting attention. In many schools such meetings will be held in the evening to make it possible for working parents who hold daytime jobs outside the home to attend. Often refreshments are served and name tags are provided to help parents and teachers get to know one another's names. One of the positive aspects of such a meeting is that parents can make contact with other parents of young children, so that the occasion serves both an educational and a social function. One parent responded positively on my questionnaire:

> I liked having other parents who, as I gradually got to know them, I could learn from and talk with about the progress and process of being parents and raising children.

Sometimes the meeting might feature "old" parents from the prior year, who speak about their experiences and feelings at the beginning of the year. There might be a display of the work of children from past years—their paintings, drawings, clay work, wood constructions—or photographs of children during the first days. Directors and teachers might prepare a list of books for parents to read to their children or might have some books available on display for parents to browse through or borrow.

Parent meetings may be informal or formal in structure, depending on the personality and preferences of the person leading the meeting. You will be able to tell something about the nature of the meeting just from the arrangement of the chairs when you come in. Are they arranged in rows or in a circle? In most cases the circle format permits the maximum amount of interchange between participants, while the rows tend to forecast a more structured meeting. Probably the most important aspect of the meeting will be the sharing parents do with one another. Certainly you will also expect to gain specific information about the program, about the plans for opening day, and about the policies and procedures of the center as a whole.

This meeting will be an opportunity for you to raise questions and concerns or any confusions related to the program and/or to the beginning days. In one such parents' meeting, a father asked, "How does it go for parents when you say goodbye at the center as opposed to saying goodbye at home?" He seemed worried that his daughter might have different feelings about being left at home and being left at the center.

The teacher in this case was very experienced with school beginnings and gave a long, explicit answer:

Everyone has a different way of saying goodbye. You and I can talk about how you say goodbye at your house, and I can learn from you. There's no set answer about how we say goodbye here, but we do ask you to say goodbye. What we want is to make links with home before you say goodbye here. You'll provide pictures of yourselves to hang on our wall. I will send a letter to the children telling them that I am waiting to see them. You'll be talking with the children at home about the center. You'll be teaching us about your children. We have already learned that Katherine is called Katie; that Carlos carries the corner of an old blanket to every new place. We also make home visits. We get to know that your cat is black, where the kitchen is, what toys your child enjoys.

We'll ask you to stay close to the building when you first say goodbye, and we'll ask you to come back soon. Everyone will be on an individual schedule. It's not step by step. It's a process; it goes on all year. There will be give and take between the teachers and the parents.

This teacher's answer seemed reassuring to many of the parents, and they felt free to begin asking questions. Since this was an all-day program for children six months through four years, people asked questions about naps, about the various activities in which the children would be involved, about schedules for eating, for playing, for going outdoors, for sleeping. There was concern for going-home time: "Do all the children think it's time to go when the first child is picked up?"

The teacher did not immediately answer all questions directly. Often she encouraged other parents to give an opinion if it seemed appropriate, or she asked parents to raise other, related questions, and then she answered them together. In that way parents began to share their concerns with one another. They found out that they were not alone in their worries.

Here are some of the questions parents wanted to discuss:

How long will it take before my son can stay without me?

What do you do if a child cries a lot?

My daughter is used to my leaving for work. Can my sister bring her to school?

My boy has never been left with anyone outside the family. How long will it take for him to get used to the center?

Will there be an opportunity for me to tell you some things about her eating preferences and habits?

The teacher reassured the parents that if children cry a lot she tries many different ways to comfort them, including ways that the parent has used. If the situation is extreme and the child is utterly miserable, a phone call to the parent will be made. As for an opportunity to tell about eating preferences, the teacher made it clear that they could discuss this at a conference or during the first days when the parent was in the room. The questions about adjustment to the center were addressed together. The teacher emphasized that each child is different and that it was impossible to know how much time would be needed for a particular child to feel comfortable and safe. She added that the parent's sister could certainly bring the child to school but suggested that the parent come along, too, at least for a short time the first day. The mother's presence, even though brief, would convey to her son that she approved of this center.

If the school or center you have chosen has a plan for the beginning that includes such features as a home visit, a gradual and staggered entry, a slow-paced phasing-in period, an individual approach to

When parents and teachers build a cooperative relationship it supports a child's growth.

each parent-child need and style of separating, a place and time for parent conferences or mini-conferences, and a general belief in the importance of this separation event, you will be supported in your efforts to encourage your child's positive growth and development. Then you and your son or daughter can emerge from this experience feeling cared for and nurtured.

Fathers and Children

Not all conferences and parental contacts arc with mothers. While the word "parent" is still largely equated with women in this society, it is a growing reality that many men are deeply involved in the day-to-day care of their children. There are those who share child care with women and those who have sole responsibility for the rearing of their children. As a father, you may find that the teacher's attitude toward you depends on the amount of experience she has had with men as caretakers of young children.

During the past decade the role of the father has started to change profoundly. Many men are exploring new ways to express both their masculinity and their ability to nurture, a combination that has not traditionally existed in this country. As one father wrote: "One of the most significant changes in fathering today is the recognition that fathers need not be bound by the traditional roles handed down by their fathers and grandfathers . . . They want to balance and integrate the provider/protector role with the nurturer/caregiver role."[3]

This shift in role has produced conflict for many men, and they often experience ambivalence about the meaning of masculinity. At the same time, both sexes have mixed feelings about men who are taking

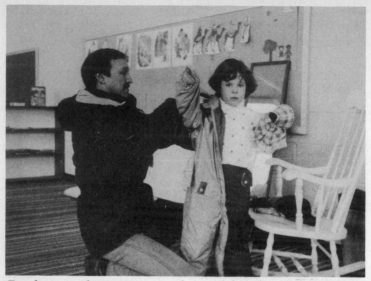
Teachers are beginning to understand fathers as caretakers of their young children.

on a new role. Caretaking men are often regarded as less than masculine, their work as unimportant.

A significant aspect of the recent studies on fathers is that children are more attached to fathers than had previously been acknowledged in professional literature. Fathers have been shown to find school separations stressful.[4] It is important for teachers to recognize that fathers need as much empathy and attention during the separation process as mothers and children do, and that fathers can be effective in helping children adjust to the new situation.

Marcus, aged four, stood outside the classroom door, refusing to come in, burying his face and body in his father's legs. The teacher encouraged them to enter, but short of dragging Marcus in, it was clearly impossible. The teacher left the door open and encouraged the father to stay there with Marcus, for the short first-day session. She repeatedly made contact with them, speaking encouraging words to the father in her attempt to help him find comfort in this uncomfortable situation.

The next day, the teacher and Marcus' father decided that he would carry Marcus into the room. Mr. C. sat in a chair with Marcus on his lap. Marcus hid his face on his father's shoulder and closed his eyes, refusing to look at the room or the teacher, who tried to play a peek-a-boo game with him. The teacher shared Mr. C.'s discouragement but urged him to continue to come to the classroom the next day.

When Mr. C. arrived on day three, Marcus was willing to walk in with him and again sit on his lap. As long as Mr. C. kept his arms around Marcus, he sat up and looked around. Although the teacher smiled and spoke to them both many times during the shortened morning session, Marcus remained stony-faced and still. The teacher reminded Mr. C. that progress had been made since the first morning and communicated her faith that eventually Marcus would let go of his father and come to school.

The next few days proved her right. Her continuing support of Mr. C. and her reaching out to Marcus allowed him gradually to slip from lap to floor, from standing next to his father to sitting at a table with a puzzle, to painting, to engagement with the teacher, and finally to interacting with other children.

Mr. C. and the teacher built a strong relationship in those first few days. While Mr. C. continued to be an important person to Marcus, the boy finally was able to transfer some of his trust from his father to the teacher.

Until recently, men have been neglected in the child development literature,[5] and thus few books for teachers have included a point of view about fathers. If you find, as a father, some hesitancy on the part of the early childhood teacher toward you as nurturer, it may be due to a lack of familiarity with the new role.

The absorption of fathers and men in the lives of young children is a trend gaining much momentum and is adding richness to the lives of all.

Ways that Teachers Help Parents

Sometimes the entry and separation procedure does not go smoothly. Some children and parents have a difficult time. These difficulties take many different forms, and while there may be elements of similarity from one relationship to the next, no two parent-child pairs are exactly alike in the way they cope. Because of this, there are various ways for teachers to help parents through this time.

Here is the way a teacher helped Maria's mother:

Ms. G. was clearly shocked and angry when her child screamed and cried as she attempted to leave her in the center. "I think she's pulling an act," Ms. G. told the teacher.

"Why do you suspect that?" the teacher asked.

"Well, she's never done anything like this before. She never cries or anything when I go to work and leave her at her grandmother's."

As the teacher and mother discussed Maria's behavior, the mother revealed that she had never left three-year-old Maria in any strange place before. Ms. G., however, thought it was an "act" and that Maria should straighten out and stay in school without such a big fuss. Besides, Ms. G. had to go to work and couldn't be spending long hours at the center.

The teacher, recognizing Ms. G.'s need to leave for work, supported her leaving, and reassured her that she would take good care of Maria.

"Children frequently cry and cling to their mothers when they are left in a new place. They're frightened and worried about themselves. We understand that in this center and we'll do everything we can to help Maria feel safe. We'll hold her and play with her. Why don't you call us when you have a break at work and we'll tell you what's going on here. You can talk to Maria, too. She might cry when she hears your voice, so prepare yourself.

What it means is that she loves you and misses you. But the phone call is important for her. It's a way of telling her that you're still okay and that you love her and you will be back."

Perhaps Maria's mother only pretended that Maria never acted that way because she was afraid that the teacher would not accept Maria into her center. On the other hand, perhaps she was genuinely surprised. Whatever the case, Ms. G. needed the teacher's help just as much as Maria did. Telling Ms. G. to phone from work was a way of informing her that the teacher was on her side and understood how worried she felt, even if she never said so. It is appropriate for you to *expect* support from the teacher—likewise, it is appropriate for the teacher to expect cooperation from you.

Sometimes parents become angry at the teacher for suggesting that they stay with their child, even though they know it is school policy.

Teachers can help in situations like this by being firm without being angry. A teacher might say:

I can see that you're uncomfortable here with Nikki and that you'd prefer to leave. I can understand your feeling of wanting to go when she clings to you that way. But it's very common for children to act that way at this age—we pretty much expect it here at school. She truly seems to need you and isn't ready yet to accept me. Do you have any suggestions for how I might get to know Nikki—things that she particularly likes to do and could do with me so that she'll come to trust me and feel safe here? Do you have any ideas about ways that you could help her before you need to leave?

This teacher has tried to enlist Nikki's mother in the solution of the problem and help her become responsible for the comfort of her own child. This sets a tone of cooperation and gives the parent a sense of power in the situation.

If Nikki's mother had insisted on the necessity of her leaving, the teacher might also ask, "Who else takes care of her? Might that person be able to spend some time with her in school?"

Teachers often hold "mini-conferences," which seem to take place in a natural way, with parents at drop-off and pickup time. These brief opportunities to talk together are often very helpful to parents. Here is how one teacher used those informal times in a positive way:

I have had many mini-conferences with Angela's mother in which we both shared our concern about Angela's reticence. Mrs. R. really tuned in during these conferences, and we did some good teamwork. For several weeks, Mrs. R. took Angela out of school at noon. They had lunch together and she gave Angela more focused, intimate talking time. In the classroom, I tried to give Angela the support and encouragement she needed, and she seems finally to be coming into her own. She seems to be feeling stronger about being Angela, and I think she is ready to use language more abundantly.

Some parents need help in leaving their child—like the mother who holds her child on her lap for long periods of time; or the father who leaves but continues to peer through the classroom window. Often a teacher's honesty in situations like these is a relief for parents:

You seem to be having trouble making up your mind about whether Carrie should be here or not. A lot of parents feel that way—they want their children to have a good time in school, but at the same time they feel unhappy about the fact that the children are growing up or spending time away from them. Would it help if you went out for half an hour or an hour and then came back? We could increase the time out of the room each day until you both feel comfortable. Why don't you tell me when you're ready to do that?

During these beginning days in some schools and centers, there is a coffeepot available in the hall or in another room for parents to use as they begin to take short leaves from the room.

Sometimes parents are concerned about leaving their children but are not able to share those feelings with the teacher. This might be because they themselves are shy, or because they believe that the teacher may see them as interfering in the classroom life. In order to cover up that shyness, a parent might become brusque instead. Sensitive teachers can reach out:

> Mr. L. was often directive toward Marc, telling him what to do and how to do it—"Put a nose and mouth on that face you just painted." When the teacher noticed that Mr. L. seemed to avoid her, she wondered whether Mr. L. was worried that Marc might not be looked after in school. So she asked him how he felt about leaving Marc with her. He admitted that he felt a little apprehensive because Marc is so quiet and undemanding that sometimes he could be overlooked. The teacher assured Mr. L. that she would take good care of Marc and that she was very fond of the boy. She recognized, with him, that quiet children can, indeed, be overlooked.

Once in a while, after a suitable amount of time, a child is ready to move out on his own into the life of the classroom but the parent is not. It may be hard for such a parent to say that final goodbye, leave the room, and go about her own business. "We sometimes may not be aware that it is hard for us to separate from our children . . . And this absence of awareness can sometimes make our separation their separation," writes Judith Viorst.[6] She describes a mother leaving her child at nursery school "where he's quickly engrossed in putting pegs in a pegboard.

> "Goodbye, I'm leaving now," his mother tells him.
> The boy looks up and says a cheerful goodbye.
> "But I'll be back very soon," his mother tells him.

The boy, without looking up this time, says, "Bye."

"Yes, I'll be back at twelve o'clock," the mother assures her son, and adds—when this doesn't rattle him—"Don't worry." At which point, having at last been convinced that his mother's departure is something to worry about, he bursts into tears.[7]

This circumstance is almost as difficult for teachers to cope with as it is for parents. Frequently teachers get annoyed and might speak to parents in a way that makes them feel ashamed or angry. If you find yourself in such a situation, what you need from the teacher or the director is help, not blame. On the other hand, a teacher who has true empathy for parents can really be helpful:

It seems to be very hard for you to say goodbye to Elysa. I wonder if we can make a plan that will make it more comfortable for you.

Hopefully, you will find a school or center in which the teachers can help young children and their parents separate comfortably through a variety of means. It is important for you to believe that the teachers have faith in their own ability to care for your child competently. It is equally important for you to see this demonstrated daily.

In good preschools, teachers help parents recognize that the separation process takes time and effort and cooperation. Your own understanding that saying goodbye when children start school is an evolution rather than an isolated event will influence your child's growing independence.

Nils is uncomfortable knowing that his mother is about to leave. He frets when the teacher tries to comfort him.

He returns to his mother for comfort from his distress,

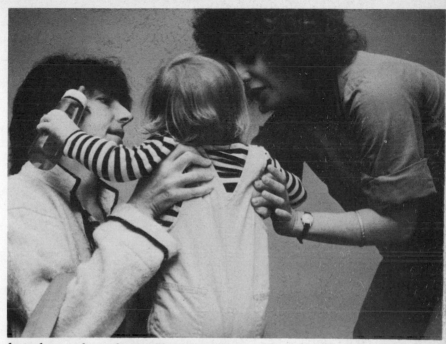

but she needs to leave. She gives him to the teacher, who receives him affectionately and with understanding.

His mother is gone.

"It's sad when a mom has to leave her little boy," the teacher says consolingly.

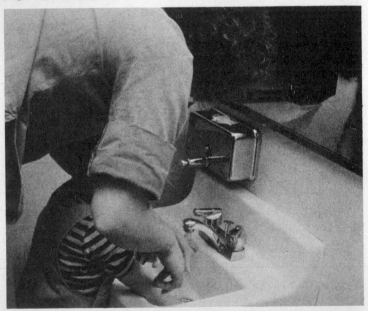

Gently she helps him into water play at the sink, reassuring him with her words and her presence.

Sample Questions for a Parents' Questionnaire

This questionnaire has been designed to help teachers know more about the children who will be entering their classrooms for the first time, and about events that might affect the way they separate from their parents. It is also designed to alert parents to the possibility that their child may need attention and care when going through this particular event. It is not a scientifically perfected instrument, nor is it meant to be. Rather, it is a guide to help teachers and parents focus upon some aspects of the child's experiences and personality that may relate to the entry and separation process. Its purpose is to sensitize teachers and parents to the possible meaning of children's behaviors at this time.

After each question you will find a short explanation of why that particular question is asked and what its use might be.

1. How old was your child when you first left him/her with a sitter or someone other other than you?

How did s/he react at that time?

How does s/he react now?

Have there been any changes in the people who take care of him/her?

If yes, how does s/he react to those changes?

How do you feel when you leave him/her with another person for care?

Explanation: This question is designed to help you reflect on your child's past and present reactions to your leaving as well as on your own feelings, so that when school begins you may have formed an idea of how it will go for you both. The answers you give will help the teacher become more aware of your needs and those of your son or daughter.

2. Does your child have a favorite blanket or toy to which s/he is attached?
Under what circumstances does s/he use it?

Explanation: Asking about your child's security object lets you know that you don't have to burn it or bury it in the backyard before your child goes off to school or group care! Ascertaining the circumstances of its use will help the teacher know when to expect to see it come out of the cubby and whether the child has extended, or reduced, its use.

3. How does your child react to people s/he does not know, either in or outside your home?

Explanation: Thinking about your son or daughter's response to strangers in both familiar and unfamiliar settings will add specifically to your observations. Your answer will alert the teacher to your child's special way of reacting to new people.

4. Has your child ever been left accidentally for a brief time, such as in the supermarket?
If yes, how did s/he react?

Explanation: This question is intended to reveal something about the child's style in a tense situation and to sensitize parents to a very ordinary form of separation.

5. How does your child behave when s/he is asked to mix with a new group, such as at a birthday party?

Explanation: As above, this question is designed to help parents consider their child's reaction to a familiar form of separation. It might provide a clue for teachers about the child's possible reaction to unknown children. Knowing what to expect helps a teacher accept the child as s/he is.

6. Has your child ever stayed overnight at the home of a friend or relative?
If yes, describe his/her reactions to the experience.

Explanation: An overnight stay is a more dramatic separation experience. Thinking about how your son or daughter managed such an event may give you some insights into the child's feelings about separation. Thinking about your own role in preparing him/her for this may be helpful to you as you begin to prepare for school opening.

7. Have either or both parents been away overnight or for a period of time?
If yes, how old was the child at the time?
How long was the separation in days or weeks?
How did s/he react to this separation?
Who cared for him/her at that time?

Explanation: This type of separation, in which the parent does the leaving, is similar to what happens when school or group care begins—but obviously, it is not identical. The age of the child is also important here, as is the length of time the parent was away, because the younger the child, the longer the separation appears to be. Recollection about reactions to events like this tell you some important information about your child's coping style—and probably something about yourself, too.

8. Has your child ever been hospitalized?
If yes, at what age?

For what reason?

For what length of time?

Were you allowed to stay with your child? In the day only or overnight?

Describe the circumstances, including his/her reactions to this hospitalization.

How did s/he behave when s/he came home?

Explanation: When a child goes to the hospital, the separation is compounded by the family's anxiety about the illness itself and the child's ability to understand what is happening. The way children express their feelings about this frightening experience affects their psychological well-being. Recent research shows that children who express their negative reactions cope better than those who suffer their anger and fear in silence or compliance. Older studies have found that children also do better when their parents are able to stay with them; many hospital pediatric units provide beds or comfortable chairs for that purpose.

When children return home from the hospital, even if parents have been able to stay with them, they may continue to be negative, anxious or fearful. One child I know whose mother stayed overnight with her played, upon returning home, a game called "broken leg" every day for months. In her hospital room had been two little girls with broken legs in traction. Her upset about her own hospital experience (which had nothing to do with broken legs) took the tangible form of these girls' disabilities. Her repeated play seemed to provide the balm needed to soothe her anxious feelings.

This question about hospitalization is posed to give you the opportunity to reflect on your child's way of coping with it. Such information is important for teachers to have because it may have some effect on your child's ability to leave you when school starts, especially if the hospitalization was a recent happening. This disclosure means that you and the teacher can both be alert to any possible relationship between the hospital experience and the new school entrance.

9. Was either parent ever hospitalized?
If yes, for what length of time?
What was the child told?
Was s/he permitted to visit
What were his/her reactions?

Explanation: There will be different feelings aroused in a family depending on the nature of the hospitalization. Having a baby is one thing, but having an operation is another. These clearly affect children in different ways. Often, after a parent has been away in the hospital, children become very clingy, whiney, or even negative when that parent comes home. Children may be fearful that the parent may disappear again without warning and/or they may be angry at the parent for going away. If this event has occurred around the time of starting school, it may affect the child's separation reactions. Being aware of this is helpful to parents, and knowing it is important for teachers, because they can then work together to make the school entrance process as comfortable and as reassuring as possible for the child.

10. Has there been a death of anyone close to your family, or of a pet?
If yes, what was the child's relationship to that person?
What was s/he told?
What were his/her reactions to the death?

Explanation: Death is clearly the final separation. While adults understand that only too well, young children often do not. They may keep asking for the return of the person or pet who has died, may express resentment that the person is no longer there, or may even wish to dig up a buried pet. These behaviors are very painful for adults to endure. Experience with death may have an impact on the way children react to other separations, including the separation of starting school. For that reason, this information is important for parents to share with teachers.

11. If you and your spouse have been separated or divorced, what is the living arrangement for your child?

What has been his/her reaction to this situation?

In what way do you think it will affect his/her entry into school and his/her separation from you?

Explanation: This question has been included for fairly obvious reasons. Families have so many different feelings and ways of accommodating to divorce that the more information that can be shared with the teacher about the child's life, the more the teacher can be on the lookout for any troubling moments and be there to help when needed.

12. Have you moved during the child's lifetime?

If yes, how many times?

How old was your child?

How did s/he react to the move?

Explanation: Moving is an uprooting and disturbing experience for even the most well-organized family. Nothing seems to be in its right place for the longest time and many people, including children, feel disoriented and dislocated. Very young children have difficulty understanding what moving means. Some of them think that their whole apartment or house will move to a new spot, or they insist that they want to take their own room with them when the moving van arrives. Sometimes they are very confused, or frightened, because the adults, in order to expedite matters, have left the children with grandparents or friends and neglected to explain carefully what was happening. It is not unusual for families to move to a new community and within a short time place the children in school. While most children accommodate to these changes, some have a hard time.

This question was included to help parents think about the posssible effects of a move on their child's entry to school. Moving is another kind of separation, from a familiar environment, from friends, sometimes from family. Children, as well as adults, have feelings about the change that they may carry with them as they begin school. When teachers know about the fact that a child has recently moved they will be more sensitive to any upset that the child might display.

13. What does your child do when s/he is angry?
Afraid?
Sad?
Happy?

Explanation: This question was included in order for parents to write about their child's individual way of expressing a range of emotions. This will help the teacher get to know the child better and be tuned into the special ways in which your child may behave. Children are more likely to show their feelings through their behavior than through their words.

14. What makes your child fearful?

Explanation: Some children are afraid of bugs, some of shadows on the wall. Others find loud noises or sudden movement frightening. Many are frightened when their parents leave them at school. The list is endless. What was scary today may not be so scary tomorrow. When you are able to share with the teacher those things that frighten your child, she gets to know another dimension of your son or daughter's personality. She will be alert to those conditions and may be able to help your child grow beyond these fears to greater security, with your cooperation.

15. How does your child recover from emotional stress?

Explanation: When you examine the answer to this question you will go a long way toward appreciating your child's strengths and understanding how he or she copes. Knowing this, and sharing it with the teacher, will be useful in appraising how well the child is doing in working through his/her feelings about separating from you.

16. How do you think your child will react to beginning school?

How do you think s/he will react when you leave him/her in school without you?

Explanation: All the other questions have focused on your child's pattern of separating. They have provided you with the opportunity to reflect on your child's particular style of saying goodbye, your child's prior experiences with separation, and possibly on some of your own feelings. Your appraisal is important for the teacher so that as you work together you can clarify or amend your ideas if necessary.

17. What does your child like to do that may help us plan activities for him/her?

Explanation: This question, and the two following, are designed specifically to aid your child's life in school or group care. They are pointed questions about your son or daughter's preferences that can be included in the school program in order to help make the transition to school as comfortable and as familiar as possible.

18. What are your child's favorite games? Storybooks? Toys?

19. Are there any special routines you and your child have established when you say goodbye?

20. What else would you like us to know about your child that would help us in planning for his/her most comfortable entry into school and the most comfortable separation for both of you?

Chapter 6

CHOOSING A SCHOOL THAT CARES

This book reflects the position that parent-child attachment is a basic necessity for healthy human development. Without the security of this attachment, children are limited in their capacity to become related human beings, capable of conceptual and creative activity. Helping children achieve a successful separation and adjustment to preschool settings is an incomparable opportunity for both parents and teachers to influence young lives. When children are able to master their separation feelings at school entry, they have achieved a giant step in their growth. This separation then becomes "a healthy prototype for all the separations that will follow."[1]

When a school or center regards entry and separation as an opportunity for growth rather than as a problem its procedures and policies will support this idea.

There are ways that you can find out the school's point of view and some ways in which you may be able to help shape it. Certainly, you will want to discuss with the director how the school provides for parent-child separation and for the child's transition to the center.

If you have a choice of preschools, select the one that has an entry procedure that takes account of parents' and childrens' needs. Reject outright any place that demands a policy of drop-your-child-and-run.

If you do not have a choice, however, you will need to be more vigilant. There may, indeed, be only one facility that meets your particular needs for location, convenience, hours, or space availability. If you are at odds with their methods of starting children, do not feel that you must "go along." These feelings of compliance often stem from our own experiences of once being schoolchildren ourselves—of bowing to the authority of the teacher or the principal. As children, we were helpless (and probably angry) when subjected to such authority. As adults we can try to amend these rules, rather than insist on changing them, provided we can control our angry feelings. If the preschool program your child will attend has no planned entry process, you can accompany your child into the classroom and sit down quietly in an inconspicuous spot. "Marylou needs me with her today" is a good explanation for your behavior for anyone who might question it.

Perhaps there are other parents who feel as you do about staying with their children to help them feel comfortable as the preschool program begins. They might join you in your respectful attention to your child's needs. Reasonable parents can have an important impact on the functioning of a school or center.

A description follows of some ways in which you might be able to help your school or center recognize that the school entrance process is an opportunity for children's growth.

A Brochure for Parents and a Welcoming Letter for Children

Many schools send the parents a short description of school-opening activities and the reasons they are held. See page 167 for a sample of the brochure one school sends to all its parents. This brochure describes the school's philosophy about separation, attachment, and beginning days. It tells parents what to expect in the classroom during the early weeks of school.

With the brochure a teacher might enclose a note, such as the following, addressed specifically to the girl or boy.

Dear Wayne,

Soon your mom (dad, grandma, etc.) will be bringing you to our center (school). We have so many things here for you to play with. When I see you, I will say, "Hello! I'm glad to see you here. I've been waiting for you."

Your teacher,

Preopening "Spruce-Up" Time

A special "room spruce-up" in which new children and their parents participate with the teacher before school officially opens is a wonderful opportunity for parents to get to know one another and the teacher, and for the children to begin to get familiar with the room and the other boys and girls. While such an event is well suited to parent co-ops and nursery schools, it would probably not be as suitable for ongoing day-care settings.

A school might set aside one or more mornings and/or evenings for such activities to accommodate all parents who wish to attend. Teachers, parents, and children can work together setting playthings on shelves, washing or painting (using washable paint) pieces of equipment, readying tables and chairs, or performing other maintenance tasks. This would provide a sense of belonging for both parents and children and would contribute to an enthusiastic opening day.

Visits Before School Begins

A school might close for a day, or part of a day, in the spring to welcome children who will be attending the following fall to visit with their parents. This gives children a taste of the fun that is to come and provides a familiar reference point when they arrive for the first day in the fall. It enables parents to talk about the school with their child as they anticipate the first day. Parents, too, enjoy feeling familiar with a situation they are about to enter.

Preopening-day visits can also be made in the fall before school officially starts. One school makes an appointment with each child and parent before opening day so the newcomers can become acquainted with the room and the teacher. Children choose cubbies for clothing and belongings, and the teacher labels them with their names.

Here is the way one public school helps kindergarteners toward a smooth entry. The school administrator sent the following notice to parents in August concerning the bus schedule for the coming year:

Kindergarten: On Tuesday, September 1, each kindergarten teacher will be in the classroom from 1:00 to 3:00 P.M. Parents are invited to bring children to meet their teachers. There will also be a school bus and driver at the school during the same hours for your child's familiarization.

Some of these suggestions are not suitable for day-care centers. However, children can be brought for a short stay on the first day either by a parent or the person who has been caring for them. Many centers find that a slow start and the gradual addition of time over a period of a few days make a big difference in the comfort of children and the security of their parents.

A preopening visit does not replace the visits that you need to make when searching for an appropriate child care facility, be it nursery school, day-care center, or family day-care home.

Parents' Meeting Before School Opens

By including such a meeting before the start of the preschool program, as described in Chapter 5, the school or center provides parents with an important opportunity to express their feelings about the entry process and to obtain answers to their questions. It is also a time when parents can meet and talk to other parents about mutual concerns and interests.

Home Visits

A teacher's visit to the home is sometimes part of a school's opening procedure. It is seen as a way of helping the child feel more comfortable with the teacher. Plans for such a visit should include the provision for parents to say no. Some parents do not feel comfortable about a teacher's visit. They may worry about their home's presentability or the teacher's possible rejection of their child if he or she does not behave properly. Others, however, may welcome the visit as a special occasion when they and their son or daughter can become acquainted with the teacher. Children may use the visit to show the teacher their favorite toys, or their family pet. This can create a special link between home and school that contributes to the child's comfort in the classroom.

Some home visits are arranged before the program begins, some take place after the program has started. As a variation on the home visit, a teacher in one school took small groups of children, throughout the school year, to each of the children's homes for juice and snacks, by prearrangement with parents. All the children's homes were visited and working parents were able to plan in advance to be present.

Most children love to have their teachers visit and often talk about it even at the end of the school year.

A Slow Beginning

Centers and schools frequently offer shortened hours on the first few days, with sessions gradually lengthened during the first week or two. Returning children may generally require less time to settle in than first-time children, although this is not always the case. Certainly children three and under need a more gradual entry than children of four and five.

As you plan for the entry, take into account your child's previous experience: Has he or she been in group care before? Was that separation successful?

Has the child been at home with a substitute caretaker? Does he or she have experience in activities outside the home?

In a day-care setting it is most likely that a core of children will remain with the teacher when new children arrive. While often these "old" children offer help to the newcomers, it is the teacher's responsibility to provide security and comfort to the new child and reassurance to parents who will be gone long hours and have limited time to spend at the center. It is best to start the child for a part day at first, adding the lunch and nap after some familiarity with the program has been established. Such an arrangement works best in family day care as well. It is also important that you give the teacher a phone number where you can be reached—and that your child knows about it.

In a school where all the children enter at the same time another arrangement may be made, not only shortening the hours for the first few days, but also dividing the group so that fewer children and parents attend together. For example, half the group might come from 8:30 to 10:00 and the other half from 10:30 to 12:00. After two or three days, the whole group might come for the full session. There are many variations on this theme. The shorter hours and smaller groups make for an uncrowded classroom and an opportunity for children, parents, and teacher to have more intimate access to one another. It provides a calm and relaxed beginning for all.

Children's Adjustment to Eating and Sleeping in the Center

If the program includes lunch and a nap for very young children, these activities are often best added one at a time. Because sleeping and eating are potent reminders of home, young children's feelings are often strongly aroused at those times. If parents are able to accompany children when they eat and nap in school for the first time it will ease the children's anxiety. Often children are afraid to sleep in an unfamiliar setting. Perhaps they are reluctant to relinquish the control they have while they are awake. Many children need to feel very safe before they give up that control and fall asleep.

A preschool setting that acknowledges the special nature of food and sleep in the lives of young children will do much toward facilitating their growth toward independent functioning.

Parents in the Classroom

When a school, center, or day-care home requires that parents stay with their children during the beginning days, parents, children, and teachers can jointly attend to the work of separating. Such a plan attaches dignity and importance to starting school and resolves for parents any ambivalence they might have about whether or not they should stay. Adult-sized chairs in the classroom, a pot of coffee in the hall, a room where parents can go as they begin to leave the classroom for short intervals are the hallmarks of a program that has planned carefully for school opening.

Once you are in the classroom with your child you

will need to make some decisions: Should you sit in the activity area with your son or daughter or on the periphery where you can watch without being immediately involved in the child's play? What will you say to your child when you decide to leave the room for a short break or a long one?

It is important to tell your child the truth. "Mom is leaving now. I'm going to the coffee room and I'll be back in a half hour, right after the teacher finishes reading a story," or "Dad is going now. When you wake up from your nap, I will be back to take you home." Suppose your child wants to go with you? If you are just going into another room, it might be reassuring for the child to see where that room is and to know that she can go there when she feels the need. On the other hand, if you are going to work and it is not possible for the child to go too, then honesty is crucial. "I know you'd like to leave with me, but I'm going to work and the teacher will take good care of you while I'm gone. I'll be back after your afternoon snack—you can count on that." It is essential that you work out these arrangements with the teacher so that she can support you and the child at these times.

"Sneaking Out"

You might feel like "sneaking out" while your child is absorbed in some activity in the preschool room. Sometimes teachers even encourage this or comply with a parent's request to do so. Why? I suspect that it relieves both parent and teacher of the responsibility—and the pain—of saying goodbye. It may be easier to avoid a problem than to face it. All of us, at times, harbor a bit of the "coward" within us.

Yet in most cases, when a parent disappears without telling a child, the son or daughter senses the parent's absence quickly. How do children feel when they believe that a protecting parent is nearby, only to discover that he or she is missing? Abandoned? Fearful? Untrusting? These feelings are hardly a firm foundation on which to begin a new experience. Consider the impact of this situation on a child's perception of you, the parent, and on the child's perception of the teacher who has allowed this to happen. It is the responsibility of the teacher to bring a parent back into the room and explain, outside of the child's presence, that sneaking out is detrimental to the child's adjustment to school and to the parent-child relationship. A quality preschool program will make it clear to parents right from the start that sneaking out is not permitted for these reasons.

As an adult you can probably understand children's feelings. For example, if a dentist told you he would be pulling a tooth, you would probably prepare yourself. If he started to pull it without telling you, you might be even more fearful. In addition, you might feel deceived. When you are told the truth, you are able to mobilize yourself to deal with the situation, no matter how difficult it is. In the coping you gain self-esteem.

It is similar for children. Having to deal with a painful event, and doing it successfully, brings gratification. When a child and parent say goodbye, the child and perhaps the parent may suffer some pain. The child, who then struggles to overcome the pain, who finally, with the parent's and teacher's support, adjusts to school, takes a giant step toward self-confidence, self-reliance, and trust, and gains a large measure of self-control. When a parent sneaks out, however, his or her child is denied the opportunity to achieve such control.

Security Objects

As a parent, you may be reluctant, or embarrassed, to arrive on the first day with your child holding fast to a well-loved, shredded diaper. Blankets, teddy bears, worn scraps of diapers, parent's handkerchiefs, nursing bottles, and other such treasures are standard fare to which preschool children cling. A center that smiles on these "transitional objects" says in effect, "We know how it is when you're two, three, four, or five." It surely must feel comforting to young children when a teacher welcomes the stuffed animals and blankets, allows children access to them at any time, and does not insist that they be shared.

A Final Parent-School Get-Together

Just as school procedure acknowledges the importance of separation from the parents at entry, it can, at the close of school, also acknowledge the importance of separation from the school, the teachers, and the other children. Partings should be regarded as significant events in the lives of all who have been intimately connected to one another during the school year. Sometimes parents join teachers and children in planning an end-of-year event that includes activities for both children and adults and gives an essence of formality to saying goodbye, be it just for the summer, or "forever."

If your child attends a center that operates year round and there is no specific ending day, there should be some form of recognition of a child's last day. Perhaps this might be a classroom party or a special lunch in which the parent participates. A Saturday party or a picnic supper might be arranged to mark the occasion.

Sometimes teachers make a booklet for departing children about their days in the center. It might include photos of the child engaged in a favorite activity or a photo of the whole group, or drawings by other children as gifts from them. Such mementos help provide an ending for the present experience. Likewise, a small gift made or purchased by the child to give to the teacher helps to mark the importance of their friendship and their year together. Ceremonies help many people feel that closure has been made before they go on to something new.

What Happens When a Child Is Not Ready for Group Life?

It is important to consider, finally, children who demonstrate that they are not ready to leave home and enter into group life with other children. These children may be unable to engage themselves with materials or enter into activities; they may be unable to respond to comfort offered by teachers; they may be unable to respond joyfully to the events and people in the program. This is a very stressful situation for parents. What can you expect a school or center to offer you under such circumstances?

Flexibility on the part of the center will serve you and your child best. The center will have to consider the needs of the particular parent and child in relation to the needs of the group—can the teacher truly give the anxious child the amount of help required while also meeting the needs of the other children? The teacher will have to make a decision about the child's potential for growth. Since there is no sure scientific measure available, she will need to make the most professional judgment possible. Perhaps the most valuable contribution the school can make to the family in such a situation is to see that they not feel defeated or rejected. A family should expect to feel supported and encouraged in their belief that development in children takes time and that some children take longer to mature than others. If the situation is extreme, referral to psychological counseling may be indicated.

The Value of Preschool Support at School Entrance

It would be wonderful if all separations could be like this:

Kim's mom says goodbye at the door. Kim is standing with her back to her mother and the door, staring off into space. Hearing her mom's goodbye, she quickly turns and hugs her leg. Kim's mom stoops down, and Kim climbs into her lap. "I don't want you to go," Kim says in a quiet voice, peering intently into her mother's face. Her mom whispers in her ear, and Kim cheerily replies. "Okay. Have a good day." The mom stands up and Kim slides quickly behind her back doing a peek-a-boo movement as she breaks into a giggle. Her mom tells her she has to go. Kim asks earnestly, "What time are you coming?" Her mom reassuringly answers, "Three o'clock on the dot—after your afternoon snack." Her mom leaves, and Kim skips over to the easel and begins to paint.

However, we know that we cannot expect partings to be like this for all children. Yet parents and teachers

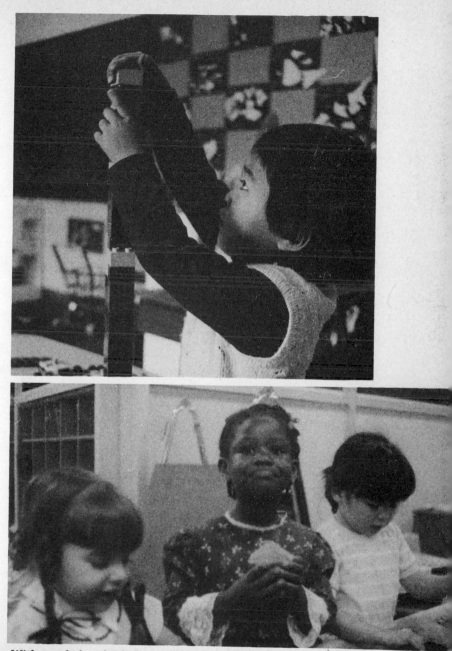

With our help, children can evolve as confident, competent and self-assured.

have a wonderful opportunity to contribute to the growth of all children who enter preschool classrooms and to help them become truly self-reliant. Self-reliance in the fullest sense is based on the knowledge that children are not alone but that "standing behind them, there are one or more trusted persons who will come to their aid should difficulties arise."[2] The mark of the truly self-reliant person is "a capacity to rely trustingly on others when occasion demands and to know on whom it is appropriate to rely."[3]

In schools where teachers and parents work together, where procedures and practice teach separation, more children will evolve as Kim did—confident, competent, and self-assured.

SAMPLE PRESCHOOL BROCHURE ON ADJUSTMENT

The Phasing-in or Adjustment Period

In order to encourage a comfortable, secure adjustment to the preschool environment, all children and parents will participate in a gradual phasing-in period during the first week or so of school.

The Importance of Gradual Adjustment

Parents, most frequently mothers, are the most important people in children's lives. The most difficult part of entering a nursery school is leaving mother. It means learning that when mother leaves, she is not gone forever.

Letting go of someone loved arouses strong feelings in everyone. Children in the preschool years are learning to cope with these feelings. Seemingly babyish behavior is a clue to these feelings. It is normal for children to express these feelings as they gradually separate from the mother and establish a tie with the teacher. Separation also involves learning to differentiate the familiar from the strange. This growing ability to differentiate is the root of all learning, including reading.

When parents invest time and effort in the adjustment

163

period, they promote the emotional and intellectual development of their children. They join with the staff of a nursery school in contributing to the children's happiness, the children's good feelings about themselves, and their continuous growth.

Some people think their children do not need special help to make a good start. Neither parents nor staff should take a chance.

Children will have different timetables of adjustment depending on their age, previous experience with separation, and individual reaction to change. Parents should not feel embarrassed if their child takes a little longer than the other children to adjust.

Preparations for the Adjustment Period

Prior to the first day of attendance or at the time of registration, parents should bring their children to the nursery school for a brief visit as an initial introduction to the school and the teachers.

Shortly before your child will enter school, it is helpful to talk to him/her about the center as a place where children go to play, learn, eat, and rest. Children need to understand clearly that they continue to live at home and that at the end of the school day, the parent will always come for them.

Parents must carefully follow the schedules for the adjustment period and the regular school term. It is vital never to disappoint children by failing to return when scheduled during the adjustment period or later when the child attends the program regularly. If prevented by unforeseen circumstances from returning at the promised time, the parent should telephone the center. It is also helpful for the parents to become better acquainted with the adjustment process by reading the literature made available by the center and by attending any meetings or conferences set up for the purpose of discussing the adjustment period.

The Adjustment Period

Toddlers Children attending toddler groups must be given special consideration during their initial participation in the program. All mothers (or fathers or babysitters) must be prepared to remain with their children. During the first week of attendance, the children will come for one half of their regularly scheduled class time. The total class register will be divided in half with half of the group attending from 10:00 to 10:40 A.M. and the other half attending from 10:50 to 11:30 A.M. The shortened schedule will assist the children in making a gradual adjustment to their playmates and their teachers.

The second and third weeks will be spent on a full-time schedule with parents in the room. Parents may begin to leave for short periods. Teachers and parents will work closely together.

Preschoolers Children attending the preschool program will be assisted in making the adjustment to their school environment by a gradual phasing-in period during the first week of school in September. For the first two days, parents will be encouraged to attend school with their children for half of their regularly scheduled time. The preschool class will be divided into two groups. Eight children will attend from 9:00 to 10:15 A.M. and the second half of the class will attend from 10:30 to 11:45 A.M. Special preparations will be made so that parents can be seated in one section of the room while the children participate in the scheduled activities. Another room has been set aside for parents as they begin to leave the room for short periods. When the teacher and the parent agree that the child is ready, the parent will advise her child that she is leaving but that she will return after work.

Children will begin their normal schedule of classes after the first week.

Kindergarten Kindergarten children who have never attended school prior to this program will be scheduled to follow a phasing-in procedure. The period of adjustment will extend over a one-week period. Parents will be encouraged to remain with their children for two days both within the classroom and on the school premises. The parent and teacher will decide together when the parent will tell the child that she is leaving and that she will return to pick him/her up after lunch. During the first few days of phasing-in children will leave with their parents after lunch.

Extended Adjustment Periods

Any children who demonstrate difficulty with scheduling or separation will be placed on a period of extended phasing in. Adjustment difficulties will be discussed with parents so that they can be handled on an individualized basis according to the needs of the child. Every possible assistance will be given to facilitate this process.

Any child admitted to a program during the semester will also follow the phasing-in procedures stated above.

It is essential never to "slip away" from children, regardless of their age. This destroys their sense of trust and may lead to difficult behavior at home, as well as in the nursery school. Children should not be prevented from crying. Threats, even little ones, will not help and will increase the worry and upset.

In some cases, it may be helpful for the parent to leave a scarf or other personal belonging. Such an item may need to be left for a long time as a "comforter."

It is not necessary to push children into group activities. Parents need to know that children usually adjust to the teacher first. As a new trust relationship develops, the child becomes interested in activities and gradually makes friends with other children in the group.

A good beginning, as well as continuing adjustment to the preschool, depends on cooperation and adjustment policies and practices. This requires open communication between parents and the center staff and a sharing in the understanding of the children. The staff of the nursery school can learn from parents just as parents can learn from the staff.

If you have any questions, please call.

SAMPLE ENTRY BROCHURE: INFANT/TODDLER CENTER

Beginnings: A Bridge Between Home and Center

We begin the year in a slow and gradual way. In this way the new children will have as much time as they need for learning to trust the teachers. The returning children will be able to reaccustom themselves to the ways of the center and build relationships with new staff members. This is a deeply important process. It is the foundation of the whole year's experience at the center for both new and returning children. It can be accomplished well only with parents present. For this reason, we ask that parents make arrangements to spend much time at the center in the first weeks and to communicate closely with the teachers about the children's ways and feelings.

In the first week all children will come on their enrolled days for an hour and a half. This abbreviated schedule will permit the staff, children, and parents to meet in very small groups to begin to get to know each other. The teachers will watch carefully as you care for your child in order to learn what your child is like and the kind of care he/she is used to. You will have an opportunity during these brief sessions to ask questions and give information. This is also an important time for the staff to get to know you and your child.

This schedule may also allow the staff to begin to make

167

brief (no more than half an hour) home visits as a way of forging closer links between home and center. Visits will take place over a period of several weeks and will be arranged on an individual basis. If a home visit is not comfortable for you, there is no pressure to have one. Please be sure to share your thoughts about this with the head teacher.

Any questions you may have about the beginning days and the schedule can be brought up and discussed at the first parents' meeting.

REFERENCE NOTES

For full titles, see References on pages 172–176.

Chapter 1
1. Ziegler, 1985, p. 12.
2. Erikson, 1963.
3. Bell, 1970.
4. Mahler, Pine & Bergman, 1975.

Chapter 2
1. Collins, 1986, p. 30.
2. Ainsworth, Bell & Stayton, 1974.
3. Ibid.
4. Bowlby, 1969, p. 228.
5. Mahler, Pine & Bergman, 1975.
6. Stern, 1985.
7. Klaus, M. & Klaus, P., 1985.
8. Schaffer & Emerson, 1964.
9. Greenacre, 1957.
10. Mahler, Pine & Berman, 1975.
11. Ibid.
12. Resch, 1975; Rodriguez & Hignett, 1981.
13. Resch, 1975.
14. Mahler, Pine & Bergman, 1975.

169

15. Kaplan, 1978, p. 35.
16. Viorst, 1986, p. 222.

Chapter 3
1. Cohen & Stern, with Balaban, 1983, p. 5.
2. Speers, McFarland, Arnaud & Curry, 1971.
3. Curry & Tittnich, 1972, p. 13.
4. Menninger, 1942, p. 19–20, quoted from *The New Yorker*, July 1, 1939.
5. Small, 1983, p. 25.
6. Winnicott, 1957, p. 183.
7. Paul, E., 1975, p. 40.
8. Ibid., pp. 36–37.
9. Resch, 1975.
10. Curry & Tittnich, 1972, p. 28.
11. Ainsworth & Wittig, 1969.
12. Ziegler, 1985, p. 13.
13. Paul, N.L., 1970.
14. Furman, R.A., 1972.

Chapter 4
1. Honig, 1982, p. 20.
2. Furman, E., 1974, p. 16.
3. Kessler, Ablon & Smith, 1969.
4. Ibid., p. 6.
5. Ibid., p. 7.
6. Langella, 1986.
7. Lally, 1985, p. 55.
8. Weinraub & Lewis, 1977.
9. Katan, 1961.
10. Jalongo, 1983, p. 32.
11. Jalongo, 1983, p. 34.
12. Katz, 1974.
13. Selman, R.L. & Selman, A.P., 1979.
14. White, 1968.
15. Furman, E., 1974; Furman, R., 1972.

Chapter 5
1. Cox & Campbell, 1968; Rheingold & Eckerman, 1971.
2. Kaplan, 1978, p. 32.
3. Franklin, 1983, p.9.
4. Bloom-Feshbach, S., Bloom-Feshbach, J. & Gaughran, 1980: Hock, McKenry, Hock, Triolo & Stewart, 1980.
5. Lamb, 1981.
6. Viorst, 1986, p. 208.
7. Ibid., p. 208.

Chapter 6
1. Furman, R., 1972, p. 234.
2. Bowlby, 1973, p. 359.
3. Ibid., p. 359.

REFERENCES

Ainsworth, M.D.S., S.M. Bell, and D. J. Stayton. Infant-mother attachment and social development: "Socialization" as a product of reciprocal responsiveness to signals. In M.M. Richards, editor, *The Integration of a Child into a Social World*. London: Cambridge University Press, 1974.

Bell, S. The development of the concept of object as related to infant-mother attachment. *Child Development*, 1970, 41:291–311.

Bloom-Feshbach, S., J. Bloom-Feshbach, and J. Gaughran. The child's tie to both parents: Separation and nursery school adjustment. *American Journal of Ortho-psychiatry*, 1980, 50:505–21.

Bowlby, J. *Attachment and Loss* (Vol. 1: *Attachment*; Vol. 2: *Separation anxiety and anger*). New York: Basic Books, 1969, 1973.

Cohen, D., and V. Stern with N. Balaban. *Observing and Recording the Behavior of Young Children*. Third ed. New York: Teachers College Press, 1983.

Collins, G. Preparing for the first day of school. *The New York Times. Education Life,* August 3, 1986, pp. 27–30.

Cox, F.M., and D. Campbell. Young children in a new situation with and without their mothers. *Child Development*, 1968, 39:123–32.

Curry, N.E. and E.M. Tittnich. *Ready or not here we come: The dilemma of school readiness*. Rev. ed. Pittsburgh: Pittsburgh University, Arsenal Family and Children's Center, 1972. (ERIC Document No. ED 168 729)

Erikson, E. *Childhood and Society*. Rev. ed. New York: W.W. Norton, 1963.

Franklin, J.B. Conscious fathering . . . a new look at daddy. *New Frontier*, May 1983, pp. 7, 10.

Freud, A. *Normality and Pathology in Childhood*. New York: International Universities Press, 1965.

Furman, E. *A Child's Parent Dies: Studies in childhood bereavement*. New Haven: Yale University Press, 1974.

Furman, R.A. Experiences in nursery school consultations. In K. Baker, editor, *Ideas that Work with Young Children*. Washington, D.C.: National Association for the Education of Young Children, 1972. (Reprinted from *Young Children*, 1966, p. 22.)

Greenacre, P. The childhood of the artist: Libidinal phase development and giftedness. In R. Eissler, A. Freud, H. Hartmann, and E. Kris, editors, *The Psychoanalytic Study of the Child*, Vol. 12. New York: International Universities Press, 1957.

Hock, E., P.S. McKenry, M.D. Hock, S. Triola, and L. Stewart. Child's school entry: a stressful event in the lives of fathers. *Family Relations*, 1980, 29:467–72.

Honig, A. The young child and you—learning together. In J.F. Brown, editor, *Curriculum Planning for Young Children*. Washington, D.C.: National Association for the Education of Young Children, 1982.

Jalongo, M.R. When young children move. *Young Children*, September, 1985, 40:6, 51–57.

Jalongo, M.R. Using crisis-oriented books with young children. *Young Children*, 1983, 38(5), pp. 29–35.

Kaplan, L.J. *Oneness and Separateness: From infant to individual.* New York: Simon & Schuster, 1978.

Katan, A. Some thoughts about the role of verbalization in early childhood. In R.S. Eissler, A. Freud, H. Hartmann, and M. Kris, editors., *The Psychoanalytic Study of the Child*, Vol. 16. New York: International Universities Press, 1961.

Katz, L. The enabling model in early childhood programs. In L. Katz, editor, *A Collection of Papers for Teachers*. Urbana, Ill.: University of Illinois, 1974.

Kessler, J.W., G. Ablon, and E. Smith, Separation reactions in young, mildly retarded children. *Children*, 1969, 16: 2–7.

Klaus, M.H., and J.H. Kennell. *Maternal Infant Bonding*. St. Louis: C.V. Mosby Co., 1976.
Parent-Infant Bonding, 2nd ed. St. Louis: C.V. Mosby Co., 1982.

Klaus, M. and P. Klaus. *The Amazing Newborn*. Reading, Mass.: Addison-Wesley, 1985.

Lally, J.R. Feeling good about saying goodbye. *Working Mother*, August 1985, pp. 54–56.

Lamb, M.E. Fathers and child development: An intergrative overview. In M.E. Lamb, editor, *The Role of the Father in Child Development*, Second ed. New York: John Wiley, 1981.

Langella, F. The monsters in my head. *The New York Times Magazine*, July 13, 1986.

Mahler, M.S., F. Pine, and A. Bergman. *The Psychological Birth of the Human Infant: Symbiosis and individuation*. New York: Basic Books, 1975.

Menninger, K. *Love against Hate*. New York: Harcourt, Brace & Co., 1942.

Paul, E. A study of the relationship between separation and field dependency in a group of three-year-old nursery school children. Master's thesis, Bank Street College of Education, 1975.

Paul, N.L. Parental empathy. In E.J. Anthony and T. Benedek, editors, *Parenthood: Its psychology and psychopathology*. Boston: Little, Brown & Co., 1970.

Rheingold, H.L. and C.O. Eckerman. Departures from the mother. In H.R. Schaffer, editor, *The Origins of Human Social Relations*. New York: Academic Press, 1971.

Resch, R.C. Separation: Natural observations in the first three years of life in an infant day care unit. Doctoral dissertation, New York University, 1975.

Rodriguez, D.T., and W.F. Hignett. Infant day care: How very young children adapt. *Children Today*, 1981, 10: 10–12.

Schaffer, H.R., and D.E. Emerson. The development of social attachments in infancy. *Monographs of the society for research in child development*, Serial No. 94, 24, 3, 1964.

Selman, R.L., and A.P. Selman. Children's ideas about friendship: A new theory. *Psychology Today*, October, 1979, pp. 71–80, 114.

Small, F. "Give me to warble spontaneous songs . . .": Using spontaneity to develop a therapeutic music program. Master's thesis. Bank Street College of Education, 1983.

Speers, R.N., M.B. McFarland, S. Arnaud, and N.E. Curry. Recapitulation of separation-individuation processes when the normal three-year-old enters nursery school. In J.B. McDevitt and C.F. Settlage, editors, *Separation-Individuation: Essays in honor of Margaret S. Mahler*. New York: International Universities Press, 1971.

Stern, D. *The Interpersonal World of the Infant: A view from psychoanalysis and developmental psychology*. New York: Basic books, Inc., 1985.

Viorst, J. *Necessary Losses: The loves, illusions, dependencies and impossible expectations that all of us have to give up in order to grow*. New York: Simon & Schuster, 1986.

Weber, L. Study of development practices at Spuyten Duyvil Infantry Cooperative Nursery School. Master's thesis, Bank Street College of Education, 1959.

Weinraub, M., and M. Lewis. The determinants of children's responses to separation. *Monographs of the society for research in child development*, Serial No. 172, 42, 4, 1977.

White, R.W. Motivation reconsidered: The concept of competence. In M. Almy, editor, *Early Childhood Play: Selected academic readings*. New York: Associated Educational Services Corp., 1968.

Winnicott, D.W. *Mother and Child: A primer of first relationships*. New York: Basic Books, 1957.

Ziegler, P. Saying good-bye to preschool. *Young Children*, March 1985, 40:3, 11–15.

ANNOTATED BIBLIOGRAPHY

For Parents

Anderson, S.L. "When a child begins school." *Children Today*, 1976, vol. 5 no. 4, pp. 16–19.
Gives helpful advice for parents of five- and six-year-olds by explaining both children's and parents' feelings. Lists some practical tips on how parents can help children and themselves when school begins.

Filstrup, J.M. with D. Gross, *Monday through Friday: Day Care Alternatives*. New York: Teachers College Press, 1982.
The opening essay delves into the issue of separation, its psychology, and its potential for growth. Through lively descriptions of actual situations, the other chapters illustrate a variety of childcare arrangements.

Jalongo, M.R. "When young children move." *Young Children*, September 1985, vol. 40 no. 6, pp. 51–57.
An exploration of the effects of moving, both positive and negative, on children. Offers many fresh

177

insights about helping children during this event. Includes a good list of children's books about moving.

Lally, J.R. "Feeling good about saying goodbye." *Working Mother*, August 1985, pp. 54–56.
This article is described on page 88–89 of text.

Rogers, F. *When Your Child Goes to School*. Pittsburgh, Pa.: Family Communications, 1977.
The author is Mr. Rogers of the children's television program. The pamphlet is written for parents to share with children to ameliorate the discomfort of first days in school. The tone is reassuring and the suggestions are helpful.

Stein, S.B. *A Child Goes to School: A Story Book for Parents and Children Together*. New York: Doubleday, 1978.
Presents photographic stories of a boy and a girl who go to kindergarten. Each story treats some form of separation, such as going to school for the first time, the death of a classroom pet, the departure of the teacher to have a baby, and the arrival of a new teacher to take her place. Each story is accompanied by a sound explanation of the meaning of the events to the child.

Viorst, J. *Necessary Losses*. New York: Simon & Schuster, 1986.
Written in Judith Viorst's inimitable style of down-to-earth humor mixed with seriousness, this book is a revelation of "the loves, illusions, dependencies, and impossible expectations that all of us have to give up in order to grow up." Beginning with infancy and ending with old age and death, it is compelling reading.

Ziegler, P. "Saying good-bye to preschool." *Young Children*, March 1985, vol. 40 no. 3, pp. 11–15.

Gives many suggestions for helping children and parents prepare for the transition to kindergarten. Includes a good list of children's books on the topic.

For Children

Adams, F. *Mushy Eggs*. New York: G.P. Putnam's Sons, 1973.
When a beloved babysitter leaves two children for a job overseas, their sadness at her departure is touchingly expressed.

Ahlberg, J. & A. *Peek-a-Boo!* New York: Puffin Books, 1981.
Baby sees different people and familiar sights through a real peek-a-boo hole on each page.

Amoss, B. *The Very Worst Thing*. New York: Parents Magazine Press, 1972.
Depicts the feelings of a boy who enters school in midterm. At the end of the story he feels that the worst is over. For five- and six-year-olds.

Baker, C.F. *My Mom Travels a Lot*. New York: Frederick Warns, 1981.
There are good things and bad things about mom's traveling, but the best thing is that she always comes back.

Barrett, J.M. *No Time for Me: Learning to Live with Busy Parents*. New York: Human Sciences Press, 1985.
A helpful book for a child whose parents are both working. It provides the opportunity for children and parents to discuss the important issue of separation and reunion.

Barkin, C., & James, E. *I'd Rather Stay Home*. Milwaukee, Wis.: Raintree Publishers, 1975.
A photographic story of a boy in a class of ethnically diverse children who overcomes his fear of starting school.

Berenstain, S.& J. *The Berenstain Bears Go to School*. New York: Random House, 1978.
The bears go to school and find out what a good time they can have there.

Bizen, B. *First Day in School*. Garden City, N.Y.: Doubleday, 1972.
This photographic story shows a multicultural group of city children in their first day of kindergarten, feeling sad, frightened, and eventually happy and engaged in play.

Blue, R. *I Am Here: Yo Esto Aqui*. New York: Franklin Watts, 1971.
A young Puerto Rican girl must adjust to a new school, a new country, and a new language. She is helped by a warm assistant teacher who speaks Spanish.

Bradman, T. & Browne, E. *Through My Window*. Morristown, N.Y.: Silver Burdett, 1986.
Jo, the child of an interracial couple, has to stay in bed for a day. Her dad looks after her while her mom goes to work. Jo waits all day for her mom to return with a special surprise.

Bram, E. *I Don't Want to Go to School*. New York: Greenwillow Books, 1977.
Jennifer uses some stalling techniques because she is reluctant to go to kindergarten. Her patient and understanding mother helps her.

Brand, J. & Gladstone, N. *My Day Care Book*. Mt. Ranier, Md: Gryphon House, 1985.
Beautiful photographs show multiethnic children and the ways they spend their day in a loving center.

Brown, M.B. *Benjy's Blanket*. New York: Franklin Watts, 1962.
Benjy grows from holding on to his baby blanket to starting to forget it. He then resolves to give it to the new crying kitten next door.

Brown, M.W. *Goodnight, Moon*. New York: Harper & Row, 1947.
A bunny ritually says goodnight to many objects in the bedroom, making the separation a comfortable transition from the active daytime world into the dark, quiet sleeping world. Bit by bit, the room gets darker as the bunny settles down to sleep.

Brown, M.E. *The Runaway Bunny*. New York: Harper & Row, 1972.
The familiar story of a little bunny who wants to run away. Fortunately, his mother won't let him. Written in a repeating pattern, this is a reassuring story of a mother's love and stability.

Burningham, J. *The Blanket*. New York: Thomas Y. Crowell, 1975.
For the very youngest children, this book shows the depth of the attachment to the security object, the upset at its possible loss, and the relief at its return.

Burningham, J. *The School*. New York: Thomas Y. Crowell, 1975.
A little boy tells about the things he does in school. Simple text and drawings.

Calmenson, S. *The Kindergarten Book*. New York: Grosset & Dunlap, 1983.

Four short stories about little animals who go to kindergarten for the first time and what they do there.

Carroll, R. *Where's the Bunny?* New York: H.A. Walck, 1950.
A peek-a-boo story without words about a bunny who hides in funny places. The reader is the finder.

Cartwright, S. *First Experiences: Going to School*. London: Usborne Publishing Ltd., 1985.
The Peach twins have a lot of fun on their first day at school.

Chalmers, M. *Be Good, Harry*. New York: Harper & Row, 1967.
A little cat reluctantly plays with a babysitter when his mother goes away. As she promised, his mother returns soon.

Cohen, M. *Will I Have a Friend?* New York: Collier, 1967.
A young child comes to preschool with his father and worries about finding a friend there. He does find one and his father says, "I thought you would."

Cohen, M. *When Will I Read?* New York: Greenwillow Books, 1977.
Jim had waited all his life to learn to read. The teacher says, "It will happen." The story tells how.

Coles, A. *Michael's First Day at School*. Tulsa, Okla.: EDC Publishing, 1985.
Michael has some fears about his first day at kindergarten but the reality of the fun he has there dispels his worries.

Cooney, N.V. *The Blanket that Had to Go*. New York: G.P. Putnam's Sons, 1981.
Susi loved the big blue blanket that her mother said

was too big to take to kindergarten. But Susi figures out a way.

Corey, D. *You Go Away*. Chicago: Albert Whitman, 1976.
The simple text says "You go away . . . and you come back" in a variety of separations involving children, men, and women of different ethnic groups. A mother hides behind a blanket and then reappears; two children lose sight of their mother in the supermarket; a little girl goes to kindergarten.

Crews, D. *School Bus*. New York: Puffin Books, 1984.
Large pictures of the school bus and a simple text make this helpful for first-time bus riders.

Eastman, P. *Are You My Mother?* New York: Designer Books, Random House, 1960 (*Eres Tu Mi Mama?* New York: Random House, 1967.)
A little bird falls from the nest and asks everyone, and everything, including a steam shovel, "Are you my mother?" In the end, the two are joyously reunited in a surprising way.

Greenwood, A. *Going to School*. Loughborough, England: Ladybird Books, 1982.
Young black children go to school in a country setting. There are activities in the book that are fun to do.

Harris. R. *Don't Forget to Come Back*. New York: Alfred A. Knopf, 1978.
Annie tries everything to prevent her parents from leaving for the evening. Their calm assurance when the sitter arrives and their return prove her fear of abandonment groundless.

Haselden, M. *Going to Playgroup*. Loughborough, England: Ladybird Books, 1985.

A simple text and realistic illustrations show children what they will be able to do in nursery school.

Hill, E. *Where's Spot?* New York: G.P. Putnam's Sons, 1980.

A very simple text and large illustrations make this a good choice for very young children. It is a hide-and-seek book about a playful dog.

Hill, E. *Spot Goes to School/Spot Va a la Escuela*. New York: G.P. Putnam's Sons, 1984.

Spot, the rascally dog, goes to school and has fun with the other animals there. Hide-and-seek "lift up flaps" add to the story's fun. Separate books in English and Spanish.

Hines. A.G. *Don't Worry, I'll Find You*. New York: E.P. Dutton, 1986.

Sarah and her mama go shopping in the mall and so does Abigail, Sarah's doll. When Abigail gets lost, Sarah rushes off to find her—then they are both lost. A happy reunion takes place at the end.

Howe, J. *When You Go to Kindergarten*. New York: Alfred A. Knopf, 1986.

Illustrated with candid photographs by Betsy Imershein, this book answers such children's questions as "What will kindergarten be like?" "How will I get there?" "What will I learn?" and "Who will be my friends?" Reassuring and informative.

Hurd, E.G. *Come with Me to Nursery School*. New York: Coward, McCann, & Geoghegan, 1970.

Photographs in a multicultural nursery school setting show what children do there. This book can be used to prepare a child for school as well as to recount the joys of being there.

Kantrowitz, M. *Willy Bear*. New York: Parents Magazine Press, 1976.

A little boy prepares himself for his first day at school by pretending that it is Willy Bear who will be going. He conquers his fear and bravely bids goodbye to Willy.

Krauss, R. *The Bundle Book*. New York: Harper & Brothers, 1951.

An old favorite in which a little girl plays a game of peek-a-boo with her mother, told with a tone of affection and fun.

Krementz, J. *Katherine Goes to Nursery School*. New York: Random House, 1986.

A young girl is photographed having a good time at nursery school. This is a board book with bright photos that will appeal to small children.

Lionni, L. *Little Blue and Little Yellow*. New York: McDowell, Obolensky, 1959.

This story is about two color daubs who are friends. They become green because they hug one another and then their parents don't recognize them. A happy reunion takes place when they return to their original blue and yellow colors.

Mannheim, G. *The Two Friends*. New York: Alfred A. Knopf, 1968.

A little girl feels shy, lonely, and fearful when she enters kindergarten. When she finds a friend she feels better. A photographic story about a black child and her supportive family.

Mayer, M. *Frog, Where Are You?* New York: Dial, 1969.

A story without words in which a boy and his dog awake one morning to find their pet frog gone. They search everywhere and finally find the frog.

Osborne, J. *My Teacher Said Good-bye Today: Planning for the End of the School Year.* Cambridge, Mass.: Spaulding Co., 1978.
Includes many photographs of children preparing for leaving school at the end of the year and describes how one teacher worked with her group.

Raskin, E. *Moose, Goose, and Little Nobody.* New York: Parents Magazine Press, 1974.
A small mouse cannot find his mother and is helped by Moose and Goose.

Relf, P. *The First Day of School.* Racine, Wis.: Western Publishing Co. (A Golden Book), 1981.
Elizabeth goes to school for the first time. After her mother and brother leave, she feels a little lost. The teacher and the children help her to feel better.

Rockwell, M. *My Nursery School.* New York: Greenwillow, 1976.
How nursery school looks to the young child, told through a simple, well-illustrated book.

Rogers, F. *Going to Day Care.* New York: G.P. Putnam's Sons, 1985.
This book by Mr. Rogers of the children's television show is full of wonderful photographs of racially mixed children, their families, and their day-care center. The book is designed to help parents talk openly with their children about what will happen at day care.

Simon, N. *I'm Busy Too.* Chicago: Albert Whitman & Co., 1980.

While their parents are busy working, three children are busy in school.

Soderstrom, M. *Maybe Tomorrow I'll Have a Good Time*. New York: Human Sciences Press, 1981.

Marsha Lou's first time in a day-care center finds her bewildered and afraid. Her mother's return is reassuring. As she watches the other children she becomes more optimistic about the new opportunity before her.

Sonneborn, R. *Lollipop Party*. New York: Viking, 1967.

The fearful feelings of a little boy who waits alone for his mother to come home are sensitively revealed.

Stecher, M.B. & Kandell, A.S. *Daddy and Ben Together*. New York: Lothrop, Lee & Shepherd, 1981.

Daddy and Ben share a few days together when Mommy goes away on business.

Steig, W. *Amos and Boris*. New York: Farrar, Straus & Giroux, 1971.

A mouse and a whale are the closest of friends. When they must separate, they never forget one another. A touchingly told story.

Stein, S.B. *A Child Goes to School: A Storybook for Parents and Children Together*. New York: Doubleday, 1978.

Photographically illustrated stories of a boy and girl, each of whom is going to kindergarten for the first time. During the course of the year they experience a variety of separations. Each chapter has an explanation for parents.

Steiner, C. *I'd Rather Stay with You*. New York: Seabury Press, 1965.

A little kangaroo who does not want to leave his

mother's pouch is helped by his mother to go to kindergarten.

Thayer, J. *A Drink for Little Red Diker*. New York: William Morrow. 1963.
A little red antelope is ready for some independence but has to convince his mother. When he manages to take a drink on his own, his mother is amazed but very proud.

Waber, E. *Ira Sleeps Over*. Boston: Houghton Mifflin, 1972.
When Ira sleeps over at a friend's house, they both discover that having their teddy bears makes it easier to go to sleep.

Welber, R. *Goodbye, Hello*. New York: Pantheon Books, 1974.
Each animal says "Goodbye, mother" and hello to a new adventure. The last creature is a small boy who says "Goodbye mother, hello teacher."

Weiss, L. *My Teacher Sleeps in School*. New York: Puffin Books, 1986.
While some children are sure the teacher sleeps in school, others offer hard evidence why she doesn't.

Wells, R. *Timothy Goes to School*. New York: Dial, 1981.
On the first days of school Timothy, an endearing animal, has a hard time with Claude, the class know-it-all. Things change when he meets Violet, a true friend.

West, M. & Wingfield, E. *Talk About Starting School*. Loughborough, England: Ladybird Books, 1978.
This small book shows how playing and learning in kindergarten can be fun.

Woldc, B. *Betsy's First Day at Nursery School*. New York: Random House, 1976.

Betsy doubts that nursery school will be any fun, but a visit there with her mother and younger brother help to change her mind.

Zolotow, C. *My Grandson Lew*. New York: Harper & Row, 1974.
Six-year-old Lewis misses his grandpa, though he was only two when grandpa died. Lewis and his mom find that talking about grandpa and remembering him lessens their loss and loneliness.

Separations of a Serious Nature

Death and intimate losses are separations we wish we could spare our children. Unfortunately sometimes children must suffer the death of a parent, grandparent, sibling, friend, or pet, or the loss of a home or neighborhood. These events require special thought and consideration. Sometimes psychological counseling is helpful for adults who are responsible for guiding children through difficult emotional stress. Professional help may be useful for the children as well. Here are a few resources:

Furman, Erna. *When a Child's Parent Dies*. New Haven: Yale University Press, 1974.

Jalongo, M.R. "When young children move." *Young Children*, September 1985, vol. 40 no. 6, pp. 51–57.

Pincus, Lily. *Death and the Family*. New York: Random House (Vintage Books paperback), 1974.

Stein, Sarah Bonnett. *About Dying: An Open Family Book for Parents and Children Together*. New York: Walker & Co., 1974.

INDEX

190

Teachers: *(continued)*
 parents' meetings, pre-
  school, 122–27, 152
 parents observing, 51
 parent's worries about
  competence of, 14,
  18–19, 20
 past experiences of, with
  separation, 21
 questions to ask, 114–15
 role in building child's
  self-reliance and
  strength, 76–85, 154
 support provided by,
  when school begins,
  115–16
 working together with
  parents, 38–40, 82,
  84, 108–47, 162
Telephone number where
 parent can be
 reached, 154
Telephoning your child, 83,
 116, 123, 131
Thumb sucking, 45, 49, 84
Time, child's sense of, 4, 72
Tittnich, E. M., 46, 63
Toddlers, 3, 24, 31, 110,
 153
 imitative play, 64
Toilet training, 34–35, 87

 regression in, 46, 48, 49,
  84
Triolo, S., 128
Trust, 10, 27, 29, 78, 157

Urination:
 bed wetting, 48
 control over, 34
 regressive behavior, 49, 84

Vacations, 70
Very good behavior, 8–9,
 38–41, 78–81
Viorst, Judith, 36, 134, 135
Visits to school, preopening,
 151–52
 "spruce-up" time, 88,
 150–51

Watching parent leave, 89
Water play, 77
Weinraub, M., 89
Welcoming letters, 108–110,
 124, 150
White, R. W., 101
Winnicott, D. W., 57
Withdrawn behavior, 9,
 38–41, 78–81
Wittig, B. A., 68

Ziegler, Patricia, 5, 70